D1514823

CORAM BOY

Adapted by Helen Edmundson
Based on the novel by Jamila Gavin

www.harcourt.co.uk

✓ Free online support
✓ Useful weblinks
✓ 24 hour online ordering

01865 888080

From Harcourt

Heinemann Educational Publishers
Halley Court, Jordan Hill, Oxford OX2 8EJ
Part of Harcourt Education

Heinemann is the registered trademark of
Harcourt Education Limited

This edition of *Coram Boy* © 2006 Harcourt
Education

Helen Edmundson's stage adaptation of
Coram Boy © 2005 Nick Hern Books Limited

Introduction by Jamila Gavin ©
Introduction by Helen Edmundson ©

This edition of *Coram Boy* first published by
Heinemann, 2006

Helen Edmundson's stage adaptation of
Coram Boy first published
by Nick Hern Books, 2005

10 09 08 07 06
10 9 8 7 6 5 4 3 2 1

British Library Cataloguing in Publication Data
is available from the British library on request.

10-digit ISBN: 0 435 23342 4
13-digit ISBN: 978 0 435233 42 6

Typeset by ✒ Tek-Art
Original   illustrations © Harcourt
Education Limited, 2006
Cover design by Forepoint
Printed in China by CTPS

Cover photo: © Peter Holst/Getty Images

Acknowledgements
Every effort has been made to contact
copyright holders of material reproduced in
this book. Any omissions will be rectified in
subsequent printings if notice is given to the
publishers.

The authors and publisher would like to thank
the following individuals and organisations for
permission to reproduce photographs:

p148–50: Catherine Ashmore

The authors and publisher would like to thank
the following individuals and organisations for
permission to reproduce copyright materials:
Jamila Gavin and Egmont Books Limited for
the extracts on pp162, 163, 165, 170, 171, 172.

Contents

Introduction by Helen Edmundson   4

Introduction by Jamila Gavin   5

Cast list   6

Act 1   7

Act 2   87

National Theatre Photographs   148

Activities   151

Scheme of work and teaching resources

To help deliver the activities on pages 151–186, extensive teaching materials are available to download free from www. heinemann.co.uk/literature

Introduction by Helen Edmundson

From the moment I finished reading *Coram Boy* I knew I wanted to adapt it for the stage. Jamila Gavin's thrilling eighteenth century tale is full of dramatic ingredients – mystery, villains, humour, music and high emotion. Moreover it is a story with an important heart, a story about the way in which society treats its children. It confronts the abuse and exploitation of children and explores the sense of ownership which adults feel towards them. It also, vitally, depicts the positive ways in which lives can change when love, respect and understanding are brought into play.

In the play I focus on two characters who reflect these ideas very well – Alexander and Meshak. One is from an aristocratic family, one is extremely poor, but they have a lot in common. Both have controlling, bullying fathers, both feel trapped, both feel the need to escape into their own heads, both develop attachments to the same girl and ultimately, both are father to the same boy. They influence each other's lives without being aware they are doing so and in a complicated story, their strange relationship provides a useful emotional and structural back-bone.

As with every adaptation I do, I had to re-imagine the story, cutting some characters, developing others, writing new scenes and dialogue and sometimes rearranging the narrative. The result, hopefully, is a play which stands up on its own, but which captures the spirit of the original work. The National Theatre's production, directed by Melly Still, was highly energised and visually inspired. The set was kept simple so that the scenes could tumble in and out of each other, and the actors themselves were used to create elements as varied as gargoyles and trees.

I hope you find much to interest you in this play and that you gain as much from working on it as I did from writing it.

Helen Edmundson

Introduction by Jamila Gavin

Many people thought *Coram Boy* would make a wonderful film or television series. But, very few thought it would be possible to adapt it to the stage. How for instance, could it stay true to the novel?

Helen Edmundson, who adapted the novel into a play, couldn't include every character and every situation. Yet she succeeded brilliantly in focusing on the core elements of the novel, and high-lighting the characters which best told the story. She cleverly merged those characters who overlapped, such as Mrs. Lynch and Mrs. Peebles, thus creating a strong narrative line all the way through, without detracting from the complexity of the plot and sub-plots.

Helen, the production team and the director worked with an ingenious set, ensuring that the action could flow seamlessly. The Olivier stage at the National Theatre is enormous and the use of the revolving stage brought an almost film-like dimension to the drama. It enabled one scene to mix into another, keeping up the momentum of storytelling. The crown of uprights encircling the stage were first cathedral pillars, then a forest, then a country house and then a ship. Helen never lost the sight of the point that, while this story was about the plight of abandoned babies, it was also about a boy's ambition to be a musician. So Handel's music was the other binding and redemptive force in the play.

Now that there has been a definitive stage production, I'm sure it will liberate the play to go on and have further life in any venue, whether in a school, or on any stage. Using completely different methods, and in completely different ways, future productions can be imaginative, resourceful and daring. In the end, whether in a novel or a play, it's all to do with storytelling.

Jamila Gavin

Cast List

Meshak Gardiner/Mish
Alexander Ashbrook
Dr Smith
Thomas Ledbury
Otis Gardiner
Mrs Lynch
Miss Price
Angel
Theodore Claymore
Lady Ashbrook
Isobel Ashbrook
Melissa Milcote
Edward Ashbrook
Alice Ashbrook
Mrs Milcote
Sir William Ashbrook
Toby Gaddarn
Aaron Dangerfield
Mrs Hendry
Molly Jenkins
George Frideric Handel
Philip Gaddarn

Coram children, Governor and staff of the Coram Hospital,
Mothers, Guests, Servants, Boys, Girls, Ladies, Gentlemen,
Musicians, Hangman and others

Act One

Scene 1

*1742. **Gloucester Cathedral**. Early evening.
Candles flicker in the echoing darkness.*

*The door creaks open. Meshak Gardiner, fourteen,
strange-faced, large-limbed, tattered and hungry,
enters. He looks about anxiously and listens. At
the other end of the nave, the cathedral Choirboys
are practising. They are singing an early
incarnation of Handel's 'Oh Death, Where Is Thy
Sting',* which he will eventually rework and use in
Messiah. *The Boys are repeating the same short
phrase over and over in response to the
Choirmaster's succinct orders. There is no one
else about.*

MESHAK   *(whispering)* I'm coming, Angel.

*Meshak begins his journey down the south aisle.
He feels that he shouldn't be in the cathedral, and
it takes him all his courage to dare to move
forward – past the gargoyles and the bloody
crucifixion scenes.*

*A sudden loud burst of playing on the organ sends
him scuttling for cover behind a stone pillar, but as
soon as it stops he emerges again and continues.
He is almost there now. He can see her – his angel.
He feels she is calling to him, whispering his name
– 'Meshak'. She is tucked away in a side-chapel,
inconspicuous, but to Meshak she is a beacon –
the most beautiful thing he has ever seen or could
possibly imagine. He reaches her and stares up at*

her – this plaster sculpture with long, glowing auburn hair, the bluest eyes and the kindest expression.

Angel.

As he stares, one of the Choirboys begins a solo. The voice is so beautiful, so uplifting. It fills Meshak's head and heart. Tears start to his eyes. It seems to him like the angel's voice.

My angel.

He reaches his hand up towards her. Then, for one sublime moment, he feels that she is moving, that she has lowered her eyes to meet his and that she is smiling upon him. His breath comes more quickly. But the Boy's singing stops and the moment passes.

The organ starts up again. Meshak sinks to his knees in front of his angel, and gazes up at her as the music washes over him.

The Choir is clearly visible to us now. The Soloist, who is standing a little separate from the other Boys, sings the last part of his solo again. This is Alexander Ashbrook, fourteen, intelligent, self-contained, intense. His voice soars up to the rafters.

Then the other Boys join in. But almost immediately, mistakes are made and confusion breaks out. The choirmaster, Dr Smith, intervenes.

DR SMITH   Stop! Stop! Stop!

Gradually the Boys stop singing and the organ ceases.

Lamentable. Is this not the very section we spent half an hour perfecting yesterday? 5

BOY   It was the new boy, Sir. He threw us out.

There are mutters of agreement from other Boys.

ALEXANDER   It's the rest in the middle of bar sixteen, Sir. I think some of them …

DR SMITH   One moment, Mr Ashbrook. Where is our newcomer? 10

He scans the Choir, with a stern expression.

BOYS   Here, Sir. He's here, Sir.

A young open-faced boy, Thomas Ledbury, is nudged and hassled. He puts his hand up.

THOMAS   Here, Sir.

DR SMITH   Thomas, isn't it?

THOMAS   Yes, Sir. Thomas Ledbury, Sir. 15

DR SMITH   You can *read* music, Thomas Ledbury?

THOMAS   I'm trying to read the music, Sir. I'll be fine once I've heard the whole tune. Only it's so split up. And it's not very catchy.

The Boys snigger.

DR SMITH   Do you know who wrote this rather sublime anthem? 20

THOMAS   Mr Handel, I think, Sir.

DR SMITH   George Frideric Handel, the most gifted composer alive today. Would you like me to write to Mr Handel and ask him to send us 25 something more 'catchy'?

Pause. Everyone is looking at Thomas.

THOMAS　　More catchy?

Pause.

Well, yes please, Sir. That would certainly help.

The Boys burst out laughing.

DR SMITH　　Enough! Enough! We will finish there for
today. Work at it. Learn it.　　　　　　30

Evening chores, boys!

*The Boys let out a groan as they begin to move off,
but there is a lot of chattering and laughing too.
Thomas is pushed out with them. alexander
approaches Dr Smith, who is hurriedly sorting out
his music and about to leave.*

ALEXANDER　　Dr Smith?

DR SMITH　　Mr Ashbrook. Nil desperandum. We shall
make silk purses of them yet.

ALEXANDER　　Can I talk to you in confidence, Sir?　　35

DR SMITH　　Of course, of course. Come to my study in
half an hour.

ALEXANDER　　I want to stay on. At the cathedral.

Dr Smith stops and gives him his full attention.

I want to stay on, after my voice … after it …

DR SMITH　　Breaks?　　　　　　40

ALEXANDER　　Yes, Sir.

DR SMITH　　Hum. I suppose it can't be long now. You
have turned fourteen, have you not?

ALEXANDER　　I'm almost fifteen. I have to carry on with my
music, Sir. Even if my voice … even if I can't　45

sing in the choir, I have to go on with my
playing and I have to go on studying Handel
with you. Please, Sir, would you write to my
father and ask him if I can stay? Tell him how
well I'm doing and how important my   50
music is.

DR SMITH   This is very difficult.

ALEXANDER   I think he would take notice if you wrote to
him.

DR SMITH   You are undoubtedly extremely gifted,   55
Alexander. Your voice is the best treble
Gloucester has heard in many a long year,
and your understanding of music is
exceptional …

ALEXANDER   Music is my life.   60

DR SMITH   But I'm sure your father plans higher things
for you.

ALEXANDER   There is nothing higher than music.

DR SMITH   Indeed. You and I know that, but does he? As
for him taking notice of me, I very much   65
doubt that he would. It's not my place to
interfere in these matters.

ALEXANDER   Please, Sir. You're my only hope.

Dr Smith considers the situation.

DR SMITH   Well, well. I can see no harm in writing to
him and suggesting you might be allowed to   70
stay.

ALEXANDER   Thank you, Sir!

DR SMITH   Suggesting, mind. And you must discuss it
with him at Easter.

ALEXANDER	Yes, Sir. I will, Sir.	75
DR SMITH	Good boy. Good boy. Nil desperandum.	

Dr Smith leaves. Alexander is filled with hope. He kneels down and prays.

ALEXANDER Please. Please …

Meshak, thinking he is alone, stands up in front of his angel. He sings a phrase he remembers from Alexander's solo – the phrase which brought his angel to life. His voice is strange and rough, but the notes are recognisable.

Alexander hears and goes towards the voice. He sees Meshak staring up at his angel, singing. He watches him for a moment before answering one of Meshak's phrases, by singing a phrase himself.

Meshak looks round, terrified at having been caught. Alexander stares at him. For a moment there is a strange sense of sameness and recognition between them.

Who are you?

MESHAK Meshak.

ALEXANDER I've seen you before. Why do you come here?

MESHAK To see my angel.   80

But at this moment, Dr Smith comes back in to collect something. He sees Meshak and comes towards him, flapping his arms.

DR SMITH Out! Out, out! This is not a shelter for vagrants! Out with you!

Meshak charges past Alexander and out.

Scene 2

*Meshak finds himself on the **crowded streets of Gloucester**. Everyone is hurrying. A bell is ringing. He looks about desperately.*

MESHAK   Da? *(Shouting)* Da?

He sees a familiar face.

Where's my Da?

WOMAN   He went to catch the ferry. He was looking for you, Meshak!

Meshak looks horrified and immediately runs off.

Scene 3

*On the **banks of the River Severn**. A crowd of people – many with carts or livestock – have formed a disorderly queue to wait for the ferry. Overhead, seagulls cry. The sun is sinking low in the sky. In the middle of the queue is a covered wagon, with a horse at the front. Behind the wagon three mules are tethered, one behind the other. Across the mules' backs there are heavy-looking saddle-bags. The mules are waiting patiently, heads down, munching the grass. In front of the wagon stands its owner – Otis Gardiner – dark-haired, in the prime of his life, he exudes charm and confidence. He has spread a white sail-cloth on the ground and on it he displays the pots and pans and tools which are his wares. A small crowd has gathered to look and buy. Otis completes a sale and jumps up on the wagon.*

OTIS   Last chance! Last chance now for your pots
and ladles, buckets, string, ribbons, thread,
all your household needs! Last chance now!
The ferry's on its way! Grab it while you can,
now!   5

Two Girls pass by.

GIRL 1   I can see something I wouldn't mind
grabbing.

The other Girl laughs.

OTIS   Knives sharpened!

They pick up some ribbons. Otis homes in on them.

Like the ribbons, do you, girls?

GIRL 2   She likes everything you've got.   10

OTIS   Glad to hear it. I aim to please.

GIRL 2   I bet you do.

Otis hands them each a ribbon.

OTIS   Let's see now – Rose White … and Rose Red.

The Girls giggle.

Tuppence each.

GIRL 1   That's more than they are on Gloucester   15
market.

OTIS   I don't buy cheap, I don't sell cheap. Quality
costs.

*Meshak hurtles up, panting and pale. Otis shoots
him a glance but carries on with the sale – taking
money from the Girls. He winks at them.*

You be sure to tie 'em tight. They're easily undone.   20

They laugh and go on their way. A bell is ringing now, announcing that the ferry is in and there is a surge of activity as People prepare to board. Otis corners Meshak when no one is looking.

Where the hell were you?

MESHAK   Sorry, Da ...

OTIS   I've got the biggest meeting of my life tonight and you could have made me miss it. Why do you always, always, always hold me back, eh? 25

MESHAK   I'm sorry, Da.

OTIS   You just thank your lucky stars that ferry was late. Now start packing up. And check the saddle-bags, one of 'em's loose.

Meshak does as he was told.

(Shouting out) That's it now! That's it! If you 30 want it, now's the time!

A Man approaches the wagon with three bedraggled Children trailing behind him.

MAN   Otis Gardiner?

Otis glances up but then goes on with what he's doing.

Can you take these children? I'll give you a shilling for each one.

OTIS   Can't do it. I've got four in the wagon already. 35

MAN   And you're worried about overcrowding, I suppose?

OTIS   What I'm worried about is getting to The
Black Dog in Ashbrook by nine o'clock. What
I'm worried about is my wagon getting stuck 40
in mud because it's overloaded with brats.

MAN   I've walked two miles to find you. I was told
you were reliable.

OTIS   When I want to be.

MAN   I'll pay over the odds. 45

Otis glances at the Children.

OTIS   Well now … There's a wool mill at Downham
that asked for four; I reckon I could get 'em
to take six. And I know of a farm or two
wanting boys.

MAN   They're strong, look – healthy. 50

OTIS   I want five shillings for each one I take.

MAN   You're jesting, man! That's robbery!

OTIS   It'd cost you a lot more than that to keep them
in your workhouse for the next five years, and
you know it. Five shillings. Take it or leave it. 55

The bell on the ferry rings again.

(Shouting out) That's it! We're moving!

MAN   I'll take it.

OTIS   Meshak!

Meshak runs to him.

In with the others.

*Meshak takes the eldest Boy's arm and leads him
to the wagon. The others follow, shaking and
wretched. Meshak pushes each one inside.*

*As Otis completes the transaction with the Man,
Meshak goes back to checking the saddle-bags.
As he starts to tighten the buckle on one, it falls
open slightly and a small arm – what looks like a
baby's arm – reaches out into the air. Meshak
stares at it for a moment, then hurriedly pushes it
back into the bag and fastens the bag up tight.*

*The Man leaves. The People in front are moving
forward. Otis jumps up onto the wagon.*

Get up here, Meshak! We're on the move!   60

Scene 4

In the schoolroom at the cathedral, *Thomas has
been blindfolded and tied up with a rope by some
of the other Boys. They are spinning him round
and round and then laughing as they let go of him
and watch him stagger about.*

BOY   Wait, wait!

*The other Boys stand very still. The Boy
approaches Thomas.*

THOMAS   Are you there? Who's that? Can we stop this
now? I ...

*But the Boy shoves an apple into Thomas's mouth
so that he can't speak. All the Boys laugh
uproariously. They spin him again.*

*Alexander enters and takes in the situation,
watching for a moment or two. Then:*

ALEXANDER   Let him go.

The Boys stop laughing and look round at him.

17

BOY   Why should we?   5

There is a moment of tension.

BOY 2   May as well. We were going to let him go
        soon anyway.

BOY 3   We all had it done to us.

ALEXANDER   I know that. But I think he's had enough now.

*There is another tense moment as the Boys wait
for their leader's decision.*

BOY   Looks like the little gentleman has spoken.   10
        Come on, boys.

*The Boys traipse out. When they have gone,
Alexander goes to Thomas. He removes the
blindfold and takes the apple out of his mouth.*

THOMAS Thank you very much. I was starting to feel a
        bit sick there.

Alexander unties the rope.

        Thank you. Thank you very much.

ALEXANDER   You don't have to thank me. If they'd caught   15
        a rat and spun it round by the tail, I'd have
        done the same.

THOMAS Still.

*He sees that Alexander is about to throw the apple
away.*

        Oh, I'll have it if you don't mind.

Alexander hands him the apple.

        Thank you very much. Are you the best   20
        fighter then? You must be. My Da said, find

out who the best fighter is and stick to him
like a limpet.

ALEXANDER   I don't fight. They do what I say because my
father is the richest and my voice is the best.   25
They're scared of what would happen if they
touched me.

THOMAS   Still. I'm very grateful. I know it's just a bit of
fun, but yesterday they stuck my head in a
piss-pot, and the day before that they took   30
me up the tower blindfold and made me
walk out onto the parapet. I'm scared of
heights. Are you scared of anything?

ALEXANDER   Wasting time.

Alexander starts to leave.

35

THOMAS   Wait.

Thomas makes a flamboyant bow to Alexander.

Thomas Ledbury.

Alexander bows reluctantly.

ALEXANDER   Alexander Ashbrook.

THOMAS   I owe you my life, Sir!

ALEXANDER   Forget it. You owe me nothing.

Alexander leaves.

Scene 5

*The dingy upstairs of **The Black Dog** in the
Gloucestershire countryside. It is late evening.
The sounds of a rowdy night drift up from
downstairs. A woman, Mrs Lynch, is standing*

19

outside one of the bedrooms with a candle in her
hand. She is plainly dressed, with strong features
and an unchanging, inscrutable expression.

Otis comes along the corridor, with Meshak
following behind him.

MRS LYNCH Where have you been?

OTIS Where is she?

MRS LYNCH In there. She wouldn't walk through the door
downstairs, I had to bring her up the back way.

OTIS *(smoothing his hair)* How do I look?   5

Mrs Lynch takes a comb from her pocket and
hands it to him. He combs his hair.

MRS LYNCH It's been all I can do to make her wait.

OTIS I knew you'd think of something. You always
do.

MRS LYNCH Hello, Meshak.

MESHAK Hello.   10

MRS LYNCH He's grown. He looks almost a man.

OTIS He's grown but his brain hasn't.

MRS LYNCH He should stay back until he's needed.

OTIS He knows what to do – don't you, boy?

MESHAK Yes, Da.   15

OTIS Right, let's get in there, shall we?

MRS LYNCH If you're ready?

OTIS Oh, I'm ready.

They enter the room. Inside, it is almost dark.
There is a small bed and on it there is a Moses

basket covered with a white shawl. At the far end of the room, a very young lady, Miss Price, is standing. She seems to take fright when they come in and she clings to the wall for support. Meshak stays in the darkness by the door. There is silence for several moments.

MISS PRICE Is this him?

MRS LYNCH Yes. 20

OTIS Good evening, Miss. I'm sorry to have kept you waiting.

MISS PRICE Are you the Coram Man?

Otis glances at Mrs Lynch.

MRS LYNCH Yes. The Coram Man.

MISS PRICE Oh, God forgive me. God forgive me. 25

Meshak moves, disturbed by her distress.

Who's that?

OTIS My boy, Miss.

MRS LYNCH He's harmless.

OTIS He's gentle and sweet as a lamb, though he don't look it. 30

Miss Price is almost collapsing with anxiety and fear.

MRS LYNCH You should sit down.

Miss Price doesn' t respond.

OTIS Mrs Lynch here tells me you have a little 'un as needs looking after.

Pause. Otis begins to wonder if she heard him.

MISS PRICE   Tell me, please … tell me about Thomas
Coram.   35

OTIS   Thomas Coram? Oh, he's a kind and gentle
man, Miss. As good as they come. The next
time they're making saints, I reckon he'll be
up there. He was a sea captain, and he went
to the New World and built ships. And when   40
he came back he was so shocked, so appalled
– I think that was the word he used – by
seeing all the orphans and the little babies
abandoned on the streets of London, that he
set up his hospital for foundling children.   45

MISS PRICE   You have met him?

OTIS   Only once, Miss. He tipped his hat to me and
shook me by the hand. And I felt a warm glow
all over. And when I'd sat down and recovered
myself, I thought, 'That was the goodness –   50
that was the goodness pouring from him.'

MISS PRICE   Yes.

OTIS   And it's a very grand place, Miss, the
Foundling Hospital, all new and clean and
with fields all around for the little 'uns to   55
play in and big gates at the front to keep out
trouble. And the little 'uns eat good food and
wear fine uniforms …

MISS PRICE   And the babies … I have heard that the
babies are properly nursed?   60

*Otis looks at Mrs Lynch. He doesn' t know the
answer to this.*

MRS LYNCH   The babies go to the country to be nursed
and weaned.

OTIS	By the kindest of women. Women who know about babies.
MRS LYNCH	Then when they're old enough, they are 65 taken to live at the hospital.
OTIS	They get taught to read and write and get apprenticed to the most respectable folk. I promise you, Miss, your little fellow couldn't get a better start in this world. 70
MISS PRICE	It's a girl. My baby is a girl.
OTIS	Oh, I'm sorry. I always assume they're boys with having a boy myself, you see.

Meshak, who has been listening intently to this description of a wonderful, safe place, recognises his cue just in time and goes to his father. Otis strokes his head and pets him.

His poor dear mother was taken by the angels. There's only me to care for him. But we do all right, don't we, son?

MESHAK	Yes, Da. Thank you, Da.

Otis waits a moment, then steps towards the basket.

OTIS	Here, is she? 75
MISS PRICE	*(aggressively)* Don't!

Otis freezes.

I mean … please don't. Mercy. Her name is Mercy.

There is a long pause.

MRS LYNCH	Can you be sure that Coram will take the child? 80

| OTIS | Oh yes, they'll take her from me. All I need is the money for my services and then a little more from time to time to pass on to the hospital, so as they can keep her in the best. Paper and pens and fancy cakes on her birthdays … | 85 |

| MISS PRICE | Her birthdays … |

She fights back the tears which threaten to overwhelm her.

| MRS LYNCH | You knew this would be difficult. You must remember what we said. |

| MISS PRICE | I can't … I can't do this. | 90 |

| MRS LYNCH | What is the choice? Tell me? |

| OTIS | Now wait a minute. If the young lady doesn't want to give me her baby then she shouldn't. The Coram Hospital can't take many and there are other babies I could take instead. | 95 |

| MISS PRICE | No, wait. Wait. Wait a moment, would you please? Please. |

| MESHAK | *(suddenly)* Birthdays. |

She stands for several moments, struggling with herself. Then she moves towards the bed.

| MISS PRICE | There is a bag here … with clean linen for when she has grown a little. And a letter, explaining … It can't be right … | 100 |

She breaks off and tries again to control herself.

There's a ring on a ribbon around her neck. It was my mother's.

| OTIS | I understand, Miss. |

MISS PRICE	*(quietly)* Take her.	105
OTIS	What was that, Miss?	

She takes out a silk purse full of money and hands it to him.

MISS PRICE Take her.

Otis takes the purse and nods. Mrs Lynch goes to the bed and picks up the bag.

And you will come to me and tell me how she is?

OTIS Yes, Miss. 110

She stares at the basket and is about to lift the shawl.

MRS LYNCH No. Remember what we said.

Miss Price takes her hand from the basket. Otis steps forward and is about to pick it up, but Miss Price clutches his hand.

MISS PRICE Look me in the eye.

He does so.

Swear to me, on your son's life, that you will take my daughter to Thomas Coram and she will be cared for. 115

OTIS On my son's life, I swear it.

Scene 6

*In the **cathedral**, Thomas is standing on a chair
singing 'The Gloucester Clipper'. There is a group
of Boys gathered around him, laughing and
clapping. Alexander enters, carrying a violin and
some music. He watches and listens.*

THOMAS At Gloucester docks, so I heard tell,
Where fisherwives gather, their catch to sell,
The rarest vessel you ever did see,
Cries, who will come fishing, come fishing
    with me.   5

Chorus.

Over and under and haul him to sea,
Who will come fishing, come fishing with me.
I'm a fast-going clipper, kind fellows, cried she,
I'm ready for cargo, my hold it is free,
Come give me a rope now and take me in tow, 10
From yardarm to yardarm a-towing we'll go.

Chorus.

Billy stepped up, he was ready to go,
He clambered aboard and she took him below,
He lifted her hatches, found plenty of space,
But his jib-boom was bent and he sank   15
without trace.

Chorus.

Johnny was desperate and up for the chase,
He drew alongside at a hell of a pace,
Her foresails were lowered, her staysails
    undone,   20
But his shot-locker emptied before he'd begun.

Chorus.

Her eye fell on Thomas, so handsome and fine,
Her prow rose to meet him, she threw him a
    line,
He filled her with fishes, she begged him for   25
    more,
And he never let up 'til he'd run her ashore.

Chorus.

Here's luck to the girl with the curly black locks,
Here's luck to the girl who ran Bill on the rocks,
Here's luck to the girl who led Johnny astray,   30
Raise a cheer now for Thomas who showed
    her the way.

Chorus.

**The Boys cheer and Thomas bows, delighted to have
been such a success. The Boys run off. Thomas sees
Alexander.**

THOMAS   Robbie Keck's finest. He's a sailor who comes
in The Anchor. He taught me all the songs I
know. He'd teach me a song and then I'd get   35
up on a table and sing it, and everyone would
clap, and some of them would throw coins for
me. You'd be surprised how much I'd get. And
then one day this man came in and said to my
Da that I'd got a voice, and that he should   40
send me to the cathedral for a scholarship.
And here I am.

ALEXANDER   Yes, here you are; singing lewd songs and
defiling the house of God. Singing songs like
that in here is sacrilegious.   45

THOMAS   *(aghast)* Oh. Still. It's stopped them picking
         on me; God might be glad about that, don't
         you think?

         Alexander comes towards him.

ALEXANDER   Dr Smith says you play the violin.

THOMAS   The violin? Yes, yes I do.   50

ALEXANDER   There's a part in this piece for a violin.
         Perhaps you could play it through for me.

THOMAS   Course! I'll do it with pleasure.

         *He takes the violin from Alexander. He looks at the
         music and his face falls.*

         Oh. Well … I mean, I'll give it a try.

ALEXANDER   You don't have to.   55

THOMAS   No, no. I will.

         Thomas begins to play but quickly falters.

         Oh, that's a sharp, is it? Sorry, I …

         He tries again.

         Oops … that's that sharp again, isn't it?

ALEXANDER   Let's leave it.

THOMAS   No, please. Sing it for me. What I have to   60
         play. Please.

         *Alexander sings through the music, reluctantly. As
         soon as he has finished, Thomas plays it back to
         him on the violin. Alexander stares at him in
         amazement.*

         Sorry. Did I get a note wrong?

ALEXANDER	No. No you didn't. You played it perfectly.
THOMAS	I've always been able to do that. I only have to hear something once and I can play it.

65

ALEXANDER	So can I.
THOMAS	Really?
ALEXANDER	But I've never met anyone else who can do it.
THOMAS	Neither have I.

70

They smile at each other like long-lost brothers.

ALEXANDER	And do you hear music in your head, all the time?
THOMAS	Yes, I suppose I do. I always have a song going round in my head.
ALEXANDER	And do you see colours? When you hear different notes? Reds and blinding whites and violets?

75

THOMAS	Not really. But I'd like to, I really would!
ALEXANDER	When I hear a piece of Handel, I see colours like … like fireworks exploding in my head. And sometimes they're like rivers of colours – soft rivers of yellow or amber or grey.

80

THOMAS	That's amazing.
ALEXANDER	Dr Smith says it's a gift.
THOMAS	A gift from who?

85

ALEXANDER	From God.
THOMAS	Lawks. Is this Handel? Did you see colours then?

ALEXANDER	This isn't Handel.	
THOMAS	Shame. But did you see colours?	90
ALEXANDER	Actually … it's mine.	
THOMAS	What do you mean? You don't mean you wrote it?	
ALEXANDER	I did.	
THOMAS	You wrote it? But it's beautiful.	95

Alexander smiles bashfully.

ALEXANDER	I was lying in bed, playing through some Handel in my head and seeing the colours, and then different music started to come, and I started to put the colours together in different ways and I realised it was my music. It was coming from me.	100
THOMAS	You really have got a gift.	
ALEXANDER	Well, so have you.	
THOMAS	No. I can just pick up a tune.	
ALEXANDER	You have. You're gifted, Thomas.	105

They look at each other in awe.

	Promise me you'll never waste time singing those silly songs again.	
THOMAS	What, never?	
ALEXANDER	From now on you've got to work at your music. We'll both work. We'll work together.	110

Scene 7

*By a dark lake on the **Ashbrook estate**. Night. Otis and Meshak ride up with their wagon and mules. Otis brings the horse to a stop and jumps down. He looks about and listens. There is no human sound. Meshak gets down too. Otis takes a spade from the back of the wagon and thrusts it at him. He points at a patch of muddy ground.*

OTIS Over there.

Meshak takes the spade and starts to dig a series of small holes. Otis calls into the wagon.

Get out here.

There are three Children remaining now. They come out, looking terrified and cold.

Go over there and do your business, then stay there until I call you. And don't think of running off – there's wolves in this wood as big as lions. 5

The Children scuttle into the cover of the trees. Otis goes to the saddle-bags and starts to undo them. He looks round at Meshak.

Get on with it.

Meshak finishes digging and comes to him. They are well hidden from the Children by the wagon. Otis reaches into the first saddle-bag and pulls out a tiny baby. It's not moving. He tosses it at Meshak who takes it and drops it in one of the holes. Then he covers it with earth.

This is repeated three times. Then Otis pulls the final baby from a bag. This one is moving – strong, distinct kicks and stretches. He hands it to Meshak.

MESHAK Still alive.

OTIS Never mind about that. Wait!

Otis takes a ring on a ribbon from around the baby's neck.

Waste not want not. Now, drop it in.   10

Meshak carries the baby to the last hole in the mud. He stands for a moment, unable to bring himself to bury her. The baby – Mercy – makes a small gurgling sound. He quickly squats and drops her into the hole. He grabs the spade and begins to cover her with earth. Her arms and legs are still moving. He starts to retch but forces himself to go on, all his instincts, his whole being in rebellion against himself. She is gone. He drops the spade and goes to vomit against a tree.

Otis picks up the spade and looks down at the grave.

Bye bye, Mercy. Thanks for everything.

He goes to get the Children.

Meshak sinks down onto his knees, then sprawls flat on the ground. His eyeballs roll back in his head and his hands twitch. We are plunged into the strange, suspended world of Meshak's 'dead' state. It is almost like being underwater – we can hear the sound of his blood rushing and banging in his ears. Distorted distant voices and memories

rear up and fade away. Then the babies seem to
rise up from the earth and the sound of their
mothers' cries fill his head.

MESHAK Angel! Angel!

A distant light appears – gorgeous and benign, full
of the promise of release and joy. And from the
light comes his Angel. She is smiling at him –
reaching out to him. But she is still distant.

Angel? Angel, take me with you.

ANGEL Not yet, Meshak. Not yet.

Otis, having got the Children back in the wagon,
comes over to Meshak and sees him lying on the
ground in his 'dead' state. Otis kicks him.

OTIS For God's sake, don't start that idiot   15
nonsense now. Get up!

He kicks him again and again.

God damn you!

He picks Meshak up and throws him into the back
of the wagon. Then he gets up in front and drives
off. Only the babies in the ground are left.

Scene 8

*In the **cathedral**, the Boys are singing ' Oh Death,*
Where Is Thy Sting'. Dr Smith is smiling as he
conducts. Alexander sings his solo, his voice
cutting through the air. Thomas is standing beside
him, gazing up in admiration. Then, just for a
moment, Alexander's voice falters – cracks slightly

– but then it is back. The rest of the Choir join in and the song comes to an end triumphantly. There is silence for a few moments.

DR SMITH   Yes. Yes. Yes. Remember it, boys. Hold it in your hearts.

The cathedral clock chimes. All the Boys break into a spontaneous cheer.

Happy Easter!

Some of them call back to him:

BOYS   Thank you, Sir! And you, Sir!

The Boys begin to run off to collect their things and head home. Alexander turns to Thomas, smiling.

ALEXANDER   Are you ready?   5

THOMAS   Course.

Dr Smith calls out as he leaves:

DR SMITH   Talk to your father, Mr Ashbrook!

ALEXANDER   Yes, Sir. I will! *(To Thomas)* Come on. Let's go and get our things.

Thomas holds up a very small bag he is carrying.

THOMAS   This is my things.   10

ALEXANDER   Oh. Well, come and help me with mine.

They start to head off.

THOMAS   Is it a very long walk to your house?

ALEXANDER   We're not walking. They're sending the carriage.

Scene 9

*The drawing room at **Ashbrook House** – a grand and sumptuously furnished room with large, high windows. Lady Ashbrook, elegant and confident, is in the middle of a meeting with the local magistrate, Mr Theodore Claymore.*

CLAYMORE   I do understand, Lady Ashbrook, that the foundation of an orphanage on the Ashbrook estate is a project close to your heart.

LADY ASHBROOK   Next to my family, it is my chief concern.

CLAYMORE   But I must warn you that the parish officers   5
are very much opposed to the scheme.

LADY ASHBROOK   Then I will have to overcome their objections. In this day and age, it is simply not acceptable for us to turn our backs on the needs of destitute children. The late   10
Queen herself threw her support behind the foundation of the new Foundling Hospital in London.

CLAYMORE   The Coram Hospital – I have heard of it.

LADY ASHBROOK   If that is not enough to make us recognise   15
our moral responsibility then I don't know what is.

CLAYMORE   The fact of the matter, My Lady, is that an orphanage here at Ashbrook will draw desperate women from miles around. They   20
will cross into our parish to give birth simply because they know their infants will be well supported here.

LADY ASHBROOK   And that is something we should fear?

CLAYMORE   There are a great many other demands on   25
             parish funds. I believe the church is in need
             of new pews. And the upkeep of the
             almshouses is costing a great deal more than
             anticipated …

A girl – Isobel – suddenly bursts into the room.
She is thirteen years old, pretty and animated.
She is shortly followed by another girl – older and
extremely lovely, with golden hair and piercing
blue eyes. This is Melissa.

ISOBEL   Mama, it's Alex! He's here! *(Realising she is*   30
           interrupting) Sorry.

LADY ASHBROOK   Isobel, this is Mr Claymore, the magistrate.
                  Isobel – my eldest daughter.

CLAYMORE   Charming. Quite charming. And who is this
             young lady?   35

LADY ASHBROOK   Melissa Milcote – my cousin's girl.

CLAYMORE   And how old are you, Miss Milcote?

MELISSA   Fifteen, Sir.

CLAYMORE   Fifteen. Then I predict we will soon be
             witnessing an outbreak of lovesick young men.   40

Isobel smiles but Melissa only looks down.

             If all children were to turn out so well, Lady
             Ashbrook, the parish might welcome them
             with open arms.

LADY ASHBROOK   Perhaps all children would, Mr Claymore, if
                  they were given the chance.   45

ISOBEL   Do hurry, Mama. His carriage is almost at the
           door.

> *Isobel bobs a curtsy to Mr Claymore and runs out. Melissa follows her.*

LADY ASHBROOK   My son is returning from school.

CLAYMORE   Then I will not detain you any longer. My Lady, I have sat as a Justice for some years. I   50
know the lower orders better than most. It is my considered opinion that anything which encourages wanton procreation or the begetting of illegitimate children is doing them, and society as a whole, no favours   55
whatsoever. I only ask that you consider what I have said.

Scene 10

*Alexander and Thomas have arrived in front of the wide, golden-stone steps of **Ashbrook House**. Thomas is standing very still, utterly shocked by the size of the house. Isobel rushes from inside and throws her arms around Alexander.*

Mrs Milcote, an anxious middle-aged lady, appears on the steps with Melissa. Two little children – Edward and Alice – run past them to reach Alexander.

ISOBEL   Alex! Is it really you?

ALEXANDER   Hello, Issy.

EDWARD AND ALICE   Alex! Alex!

ALEXANDER   Hello, little people.

ALICE   Are you staying forever?   5

ALEXANDER   Two weeks.

Edward and Alice are wild with excitement.

EDWARD AND ALICE	Two weeks! Two weeks!
MRS MILCOTE	Edward! Alice! Control yourselves.
EDWARD	How long is two weeks?
ALEXANDER	Well, I suppose it's like forever to you. 10
ISOBEL	*(beckoning him)* Come. Come, come. Alex, this is Mrs Milcote. She has come to be our governess. She's Mama's cousin, you know?
ALEXANDER	Pleased to meet you, Ma'am.
MRS MILCOTE	We have heard so much about you, 15 Alexander. Melissa and I have been longing to meet you. My daughter, Melissa.
ALEXANDER	How do you do?
MELISSA	How do you do?
ALEXANDER	And this is my good friend Thomas Ledbury. 20 Come here, Thomas.

Thomas approaches shyly.

ISOBEL	It's lovely to meet you, Thomas. I'm Isobel.
THOMAS	Lovely to meet you, Miss. *(To Mrs Milcote.)* And you, Mrs Ashbrook.
ALEXANDER	This isn't my mother, Thomas. 25
MRS MILCOTE	Here is *Lady* Ashbrook now.

Lady Ashbrook sweeps up and kisses Alexander.

LADY ASHBROOK	Alex. Darling boy.
ALEXANDER	Hello, Mama.
LADY ASHBROOK	And this must be your friend Thomas. Welcome to Ashbrook House, Thomas. 30

THOMAS	Thank you very much.
LADY ASHBROOK	You must make yourself entirely at home.
EDWARD	*(looking at Thomas)* Why is he wearing those funny clothes?
ALEXANDER	That's our uniform. 35
LADY ASHBROOK	And how was your journey?
ALEXANDER	Fine.
THOMAS	It was the best! We came in a carriage!
LADY ASHBROOK	Really? And you've brought the sunshine with you. 40
THOMAS	That's what I said!

Mrs Lynch has appeared on the steps behind them.

LADY ASHBROOK	Mrs Lynch?

Mrs Lynch comes to her.

Thomas, this is Mrs Lynch, our housekeeper. Anything you need, you must let her know. Which bedroom have you put Thomas in? 45

MRS LYNCH	The yellow room, My Lady.
LADY ASHBROOK	Excellent. The yellow room is perfect for such a sunny boy. Kindly show him where it is.
EDWARD AND ALICE	We'll show him! We'll show him!

They grab hold of Thomas and pull him to the house.

LADY ASHBROOK	That's right, children. Careful now! 50
ISOBEL	Poor Thomas.
LADY ASHBROOK	What a sweet boy.
ALEXANDER	He's a very talented violinist. He's been helping me with my music.

LADY ASHBROOK	Do you think it's possible that those are his only decent clothes?	55
ALEXANDER	Probably.	
LADY ASHBROOK	Then we must unearth some of your old ones. I'm sure we have plenty to fit him. Perhaps you could help me to organise that, Margaret?	60
MRS MILCOTE	Certainly.	
LADY ASHBROOK	We shall all dine together today, darling. A special treat because you're home.	
ALEXANDER	Thank you, Mama.	65
LADY ASHBROOK	Cook has made all your favourites. Half an hour everyone.	

Lady Ashbrook and Mrs Milcote leave.

There is an awkward pause. Melissa gets the impression that Alexander wishes her to go.

MELISSA	I'll leave you two alone.	
ISOBEL	Oh, don't. She doesn't have to, does she, Alex?	

Alexander doesn' t reply quickly enough.

MELISSA	You must have a lot to talk about.	70

Melissa leaves.

ISOBEL	Isn't she beautiful? Don't you think she's so beautiful?	
ALEXANDER	I'm afraid I don't notice things like that.	
ISOBEL	Well, you should. And she is. And I'm so relieved that she's come. I was dying of boredom without you and now she and I have become the best of friends.	75

ALEXANDER	Is Papa here, Issy?
ISOBEL	He's in Bristol. One of his ships is due back.
ALEXANDER	You haven't heard him talking about a letter, have you? About a letter from Dr Smith?

80

ISOBEL	No. But he'll have to be back before Saturday, because you'll never guess what. *(Alexander doesn't respond)* Guess what!
ALEXANDER	Sorry. What?

85

ISOBEL	We're giving a ball on Saturday for Mama's birthday. And I'm allowed to stay up for it. Right until the end. My first ball. Isn't it wonderful?
ALEXANDER	It's wonderful if you think it's wonderful.

90

She hugs him.

Scene 11

*A sunny day. The Ashbrook Siblings and Thomas arrive before an **idyllic-looking cottage** in a corner of the grounds. There is a duck pond in front of it with a little bridge across, leading to the front door. The sound of music can be heard coming from within. Thomas is wearing a blindfold. Edward has hold of one of his arms, and Alice the other.*

EDWARD	Just a little further now.
ALICE	No peeping, Thomas.
THOMAS	We're not anywhere high, are we?
ALEXANDER	No. We wouldn't do that to you.

They get him into position, facing the cottage. Isobel removes the blindfold.

ISOBEL	Now … open your eyes!	5

He does so, and his face lights up.

THOMAS	Oh!
ALICE	It's our house.
ISOBEL	It's called Waterside.
THOMAS	Waterside.
EDWARD	No grown-ups allowed.	10

THOMAS	Really?
ISOBEL	Only Nanny sometimes.
EDWARD	And Mama comes for tea.
ALICE	Only when we say.
THOMAS	It's wonderful. It's like a house in a story,	15

hidden away in the trees and with the pond
and the ducks and everything.

ISOBEL	And it's perfect inside. Come and see.

She runs across the bridge with Edward and Alice.

ALEXANDER	*(calling after her)* Who's that singing?
ISOBEL	Melissa!	20

Isobel and the Children disappear into the cottage.

THOMAS	You know, when you said you lived in a big house, I thought you meant one this size.
ALEXANDER	You are all right, aren't you, Thomas? I mean, you're not unhappy here?
THOMAS	Unhappy? How could anyone be unhappy in	25

a place like this?

They start across the bridge.

Scene 12

*Alexander and Thomas enter the **cottage**. Isobel is waiting for them. It is almost like a doll's house, with perfect, small-sized versions of everything. Melissa is sitting at the virginals, playing and singing. The Children are sitting on a rug, playing with their dolls.*

Alexander watches Melissa playing, with a slight frown on his face. She finishes the piece. Isobel and Thomas break into applause.

ISOBEL   That was lovely!

THOMAS   It was!

ISOBEL   Doesn't she play well, Alex?

ALEXANDER   Yes.

MELISSA   It's only because I practise a great deal.   5

Thomas approaches her.

THOMAS   And tell me, do you see colours when you play different notes?

MELISSA   *(puzzled)* No.

ALICE   Look at our dolls, Thomas.

THOMAS   Let's see. They're splendid. But what   10
happened to the cradle?

EDWARD   Her doll was too fat.

THOMAS   I can mend this for you, if you like.

ALICE   Yes, please!

ISOBEL   Could you really, Thomas?   15

THOMAS   Of course. My Da's a carpenter. I can mend anything.

EDWARD   Can you do it now?

THOMAS   I'll have a go …

Thomas begins trying to fix the cradle. Alexander has crossed to the virginals, where Melissa is sorting out her music. He stares down at the instrument.

ALEXANDER   It looks so small and shabby. It used to feel   20
like a whole world was opening up before me
when I lifted the lid.

MELISSA   Would you play something? I'd very much
like to hear you.

ALEXANDER   No. I couldn't. There aren't enough octaves   25
and it's horribly out of tune. Nothing could
sound good on this.

MELISSA   Oh.

Melissa moves away, offended. Isobel comes rushing up to Alexander before he can respond.

ISOBEL   Oh, play something, will you? Play some
dancing music so we can practise for the ball. 30
Oh, please. Please. Please, Alex.

ALEXANDER   All right then. Just some dancing music.

ALICE   Hurrah!

Aexander sits down at the virginals and begins to play some lively music.

ISOBEL   Dance! Dance! Everyone has to dance!

Thomas and the Children join in. Melissa watches for a few moments before Isobel comes and grabs her and whirls her around and around so that she can't help but smile. Alexander begins to sing to the music too. A face appears at the window, unseen by any of them. It is Meshak. He stares in wonder at the fairy-tale house and the dancing Children. Then his eyes settle on Melissa and his expression changes. Her auburn hair, her blue eyes, her beautiful smile – it is his angel. And then there is no one else but her, spinning and spinning in rapture. She is breathing, living.

MESHAK   Angel. My angel ...   35

Otis's voice cuts through the sound of the music.

OTIS   Meshak!

Meshak doesn't go – he has to watch her.

Meshak! Get here before I break your bones!

Meshak finally runs off to find him.

Scene 13

*In the **drawing room**. Evening. Isobel, Alice and Edward are singing a simple song – 'Three Children Sliding'. Melissa is accompanying them. Lady Ashbrook and Thomas are watching with delight. Alexander is smiling too. Mrs Milcote is showing a suitable amount of appreciation, whilst glancing at Alexander from time to time. Mrs Lynch watches as a Servant places a tray of tea before Lady Ashbrook. The Servant goes.*

CHILDREN   Three children sliding on the ice, upon a
        summer's day,

It so fell out, they all fell in, the rest they ran
away,
The rest they ran, the rest they ran away.   5

Now had these children been at home, or
sliding on dry ground,
Ten thousand pound to one penny, they had
not all been drowned,
They had not all, they had not all been   10
drowned.

You parents all that children have, and you
that have got none,
If you would keep them safe abroad, pray
keep them safe at home,   15
Pray keep them safe, pray keep them safe at
home.

The audience claps.

LADY ASHBROOK	Bravo! Well done, all of you.
MRS MILCOTE	Very good.
ALICE	Edward went wrong. 20
EDWARD	Alice went wrong.
ISOBEL	You both went wrong. I was the only one doing it properly.
ALICE	Sing your song, Thomas.
THOMAS	*(alarmed)* What? 25
ALICE	Sing the funny song you sang before.
EDWARD	You know. When we were in the bedroom.
ALICE	About the fishing.
THOMAS	*(glancing at Alexander)* Oh, that.
ISOBEL	Please, Thomas. I haven't heard it. 30

THOMAS	Oh. I don't think I'd better. Alexander doesn't like me to sing my songs.
MELISSA	*(pointedly)* Really? I'd like to hear it.
ALEXANDER	Of course you should sing it, if you want to.
LADY ASHBROOK	Why don't you both sing one of the songs 35 you've been learning at the cathedral? I'd love to hear something.
THOMAS	Yes! That's a very good idea.
ISOBEL	Oh yes, do.
THOMAS	We could do 'Oh death, why must we sing?' 40
ALEXANDER	All right.

Alexander finds the note on the harpsichord and they begin to sing 'Oh Death, Where Is Thy Sting'. Lady Ashbrook's face fills with joy. But half-way through the song a man enters and stands in the doorway, listening. Alexander sees him and stops singing. Thomas stops too (eventually). The man, distinguished and robust, is Sir William Ashbrook.

SIR WILLIAM	Go on, go on.
LADY ASHBROOK	William! Good heavens! I wasn't expecting you until tomorrow.

The Children and Mrs Milcote have all stood – as though to attention.

SIR WILLIAM	Ship got in early. Made good time. Mrs 45 Milcote. Children.
MRS MILCOTE	Sir William.
CHILDREN	Good evening, Papa.

Sir William approaches Alexander and makes a slight bow to him.

47

SIR WILLIAM	Good to have you back with us.
ALEXANDER	Thank you, Sir.
SIR WILLIAM	Still got the voice then.
ALEXANDER	Yes, Sir.
SIR WILLIAM	Not for much longer though, eh?

Alexander looks shocked and angry.

And who's our other little songbird?

LADY ASHBROOK This is Alexander's friend – Thomas Ledbury.

Thomas gives a bow.

THOMAS How do you do, Sir?

SIR WILLIAM Ledbury – do we know your people?

LADY ASHBROOK Thomas is at the choir school with Alexander. He has come to stay for the week.

SIR WILLIAM Has he now? Well, I daresay we've got room for a little one. As long as you promise not to drink all my sherry.

THOMAS I'm more of a whisky man myself, Sir.

SIR WILLIAM Very good. Very good. Yes. And what do you want to do when you grow up?

THOMAS I want to be a musician, Sir.

SIR WILLIAM Do you indeed? And what does your father say to that?

THOMAS He wanted me to be a ship's carpenter like him …

SIR WILLIAM Of course.

THOMAS … but now he's happy about me being a musician. He says a man's lucky indeed if he can spend his life doing what he loves.

There is an awkward pause.

SIR WILLIAM   A nice sentiment, I'm sure.   75

He starts to leave.

I'll have my supper in the study.

LADY ASHBROOK   Yes, dear.

*He goes. Mrs Lynch follows him out. Alexander is
standing very still.*

MRS MILCOTE   Melissa, why don't you and Alexander play a
duet together? I think they would play very
well together, don't you, My Lady?   80

Alexander suddenly rushes out after his father.

LADY ASHBROOK   Alex?

Scene 14

*Sir William is walking to his **study**. Alexander runs
up behind him.*

ALEXANDER   Papa?

SIR WILLIAM   Yes?

Alexander hesitates.

Well, spit it out.

ALEXANDER   Have you received a letter from Dr Smith? He
said he had written to you.   5

Lady Ashbrook hurries up.

LADY ASHBROOK   Your father is tired now, Alex. You can
discuss this in the morning.

SIR WILLIAM	Yes. I have. Damned impertinent, telling me what to do with my own boy. It's out of the question, of course. As soon as that voice cracks, I want you back at Ashbrook.

10

ALEXANDER	But I have to go on studying my music. How can I do that if I come back here?

SIR WILLIAM	A bargain is a bargain. I made a bargain with you – against my better judgment, mind – but I stuck to it and you will stick to it too. Music is all very well for your friend in there, but it won't do for you.

15

ALEXANDER	But ...

SIR WILLIAM	What?

20

Alexander dares not continue.

Tinkle around to entertain the ladies by all means, but your first duty should be and must be to this estate and to the business of this family. Look at me! I do not wish to hear another word on the matter. Is that understood?

25

ALEXANDER	Yes, Sir.

Sir William leaves. Alexander turns to his mother.

Go and talk to him.

LADY ASHBROOK	Alex ...

ALEXANDER	I'm not leaving the cathedral. I don't care what he says.

30

LADY ASHBROOK	You know how difficult it was for me to persuade him to let you go at all. It was always on the understanding that once your voice broke ...

35

ALEXANDER   This isn't about my voice. It's everything. I've
             started writing music of my own.

LADY ASHBROOK   That's wonderful. It really is. You know how
                proud of you I am.

ALEXANDER   I have to study every day. I have to have a   40
             teacher – a brilliant teacher.

LADY ASHBROOK   No one is saying you won't be able to play
                from time to time – or write if that's what you
                want to do. In fact you must write if you …

ALEXANDER   It's not enough! Why don't you understand?   45
             It's like if someone said you had to lose the
             thing that meant most to you. How would
             you feel if someone took Edward and Alice
             away and said you could never see them
             again?   50

LADY ASHBROOK   Now, stop it! Really. Why must you always be
                so extreme? You have to start accepting what
                your father has said. For all our sakes.

He walks off. Lady Ashbrook's face is full of concern.

Scene 15

*Late evening. Melissa is in **her mother's bedroom**.*

MELISSA   It was humiliating and embarrassing.

MRS MILCOTE What is so embarrassing about suggesting
             you play a duet?

MELISSA   Don't pretend, Mother, please. You ought to
             know now that he has no interest in me   5
             whatsoever. And I have none in him.

*Outside the room, Mrs Lynch is passing by. She
stops and listens.*

MRS MILCOTE	Then you're a very silly girl. A very, very, silly, silly girl. Alexander Ashbrook is one of the most eligible young men in Gloucestershire.	
MELISSA	He is surly and proud.	10
MRS MILCOTE	Proud? Proud? I should say he has a right to be.	
MELISSA	And arrogant.	
MRS MILCOTE	Heir to all this and good-looking to boot? And you, Melissa Milcote, have the excellent good fortune to be brought to his attention. A lot of girls would give their eye teeth for that.	15
MELISSA	Well, I am not a lot of girls.	
MRS MILCOTE	Your whole future depends upon your marrying well.	20
MELISSA	I am fifteen, Mother.	
MRS MILCOTE	And almost a woman. I was married at eighteen and Lady Ashbrook, unless I'm much mistaken, was married younger. Your dear father, God rest his soul, left us nothing, absolutely nothing. All we have to offer are your breeding and your good looks.	25
MELISSA	You make me sound like a horse.	
MRS MILCOTE	Now you really are being silly. You must stop being so touchy, Melissa. Humiliation and embarrassment in these matters are the privilege of the rich and powerful – not the likes of us.	30

Scene 16

*Alexander and Thomas are in **Alexander's bedroom**.*

ALEXANDER   I wish I wasn't Alexander Ashbrook! I wish I'd
been born with nothing!

THOMAS   Steady on.

ALEXANDER   I just want to stay in a big room and write
music. And not go anywhere or see anyone!   5

Pause.

THOMAS   You might get a bit fed up.

ALEXANDER   I wouldn't!

*This is the first time Alexander has really shouted
at Thomas. But Thomas is not put off.*

THOMAS   You have to talk to him again. You have to
make him listen.

ALEXANDER   He doesn't know how to listen.   10

THOMAS   Did you tell him you've started writing
music? I mean, playing the harpsichord or
the fiddle, that's one thing, but being a
composer ... you could be the next Handel!
Why don't you play him your song?   15

ALEXANDER   I don't want him to hear it. It wouldn't mean
anything to him.

THOMAS   Play it to your mother then.

Alexander doesn' t respond.

You can't just give up. You have to do
something. Alex?   20

ALEXANDER   The ball.

THOMAS   What about it?

ALEXANDER   There'll be lots of musicians here.

THOMAS   There's bound to be.

ALEXANDER   I could sing it for her. I could write out all   25
the different parts and give it to the
musicians.

THOMAS   Yes! That's it! And it'll sound wonderful. And
everyone will smack your dad on the back
and tell him he's got a son who's gifted!   30

ALEXANDER   I don't know.

THOMAS   What?

ALEXANDER   I don't know if I dare.

THOMAS   Of course you do. Of course you dare. It's a
brilliant idea, Alex. It could change   35
everything.

Pause.

ALEXANDER   We'd better start now then.

THOMAS   Yes.

ALEXANDER   Let's start on second violin. Play me the top
line, will you?

Scene 17

Below stairs, *Mrs Lynch goes to the back door and
opens it quietly. Otis is there. He grins.*

OTIS   Need any knives sharpening, Ma'am?

*She moves aside and lets him in, then locks the
door.*

MRS LYNCH   Go to the kitchen.

OTIS   Not this time. Take me above stairs.

MRS LYNCH   You know I can't do that.

OTIS   I've got something to tell you.   5

MRS LYNCH   Tell me here.

OTIS   I'll tell you upstairs.

MRS LYNCH   They've only just gone to bed.

OTIS   Not scared are you, Mrs Lynch?

Scene 18

*Mrs Lynch and otis enter the **drawing room**. Mrs Lynch is carrying a candelabra which she sets down. Otis looks about him, smiling.*

OTIS   This is more like it.

MRS LYNCH   If we're found in here I'll lose my job.

OTIS   Maybe that wouldn't be so bad.

MRS LYNCH   It's taken me years to earn the trust I have.

Otis walks about, taking in all the paintings and ornaments.

OTIS   Nice.   5

MRS LYNCH   You got my message about the ball?

OTIS   Saturday.

MRS LYNCH   The players are staying on in the village for a week. There'll be plenty of trade for you.

OTIS   Now let me guess …   10

He crosses the room and sits in a fine chair.

His Lordship's chair.

MRS LYNCH   Don't get it dirty.

OTIS	What do you reckon? Lord Gardiner of Gloucester? What do you reckon?
MRS LYNCH	I reckon you had better keep dreaming. 15
OTIS	Well, I reckon that's where you're wrong. What if I told you that in a year or two, you and I could be sitting pretty in a place like this of our own?
MRS LYNCH	You think that's what I want? To sit around in 20 a place like this?
OTIS	Wouldn't say no to their money, though, would you?
MRS LYNCH	I wouldn't say no to the freedom it would buy. What's this about? 25
OTIS	Come here.
MRS LYNCH	Tell me, Otis.
OTIS	For God's sake. Just come here, woman.

She goes to him.

Pick my pocket.

MRS LYNCH	You're so cheap. 30
OTIS	I mean it.

She does so, and draws out a purse heavy with coins.

MRS LYNCH	What's this?
OTIS	This, Mrs Lynch, is what I've taken from just two of your young ladies – Miss Price, was it? And the other one in Stroud you told me to 35 visit.
MRS LYNCH	So much?

OTIS   So much. It's more money than I've ever
seen. And half of it's yours. You're a clever
one and no mistake. This Coram idea's a gold   40
mine. This is before we've even started going
back to them with our little tit-bits of
information. Very soon I'll have a list as long
as my arm of young ladies who are making
regular contributions to our future life.   45

MRS LYNCH   Lives. Our future lives.

OTIS   There'll be no more trawling around the
workhouses, no more pots and pans, no more
serving. Is that enough freedom for you?

MRS LYNCH   Don't get overconfident.   50

OTIS   What can go wrong? You said yourself, none
of 'em'll go looking for the brats. These
aren't the usual snivelling parlour maids,
these value their reputations too much.

MRS LYNCH   Even so. Tread carefully, Otis.   55

OTIS   Whatever you say.

They kiss passionately.

MRS LYNCH   Miss Price's baby …

OTIS   What about it?

MRS LYNCH   Did it live for long?

OTIS   As long as all the rest.   60

*He kisses her again. She suddenly stands and
moves towards the door.*

MRS LYNCH   I'll lock the door.

OTIS   Leave it.

They stare at each other for a few moments, then she goes back to him and they fall into each other's arms.

Scene 19

*Outside, **on the lawn,** in the darkness, Meshak is gazing up at Melissa's window. He can see her moving about – it looks as though she is practising her dancing in anticipation of the ball.*

MESHAK   I'm here. Can you see me, Angel?

Scene 20

The ballroom – splendid and shining, a feast of light and mirrors and flowers. Musicians are settling themselves into the gallery. Mrs Lynch is directing Staff in last-minute touches. Isobel enters, dressed in her ball gown, beside herself with excitement. Melissa arrives – looking beautiful.

ISOBEL   There you are! How do I look?

MELISSA   Enchanting.

ISOBEL   Do I really? Do you really think?

MELISSA   You look like a princess.

ISOBEL   And you look lovely too. I'm so excited I can   5
hardly breathe.

MELISSA   This bodice is so tight I can hardly breathe.

ISOBEL   You won't leave me alone, will you?

MELISSA   Of course not. I'll stay with you all the time.

ISOBEL   Unless someone asks me to dance. Then you   10
could just go away a bit. There's Thomas!

Thomas enters. He is dressed in a neat little velvet suit with knickerbockers and a frilly shirt.

Thomas! You look adorable!

THOMAS   I feel a bit silly.

MELISSA   It's very sweet.

THOMAS   I'm just glad my Da's not here. Where's Alex? 15

MELISSA   He hasn't graced us with his presence yet.

ISOBEL   Guests! Let's go and watch.

They rush off. In the gallery the Musicians strike up. Sir William and Lady Ashbrook appear in the doorway and begin to welcome the Guests. Across the room, Mrs Milcote enters and smiles with delight at her surroundings. She sees Mrs Lynch pass by.

MRS MILCOTE   I must say, you have surpassed yourself, Mrs Lynch.

MRS LYNCH   Thank you, Madam. 20

MRS MILCOTE   My late husband and I used to entertain a great deal, so I understand the effort involved. Luckily we were blessed with an excellent housekeeper. *(Looking across to the door)* Who is that with Mr and Mrs Claymore? 25

Mrs Lynch looks. Mr Claymore has just entered and is speaking to Lord Ashbrook. Beside him are two ladies – one, his Wife, the other is Miss Price.

MRS LYNCH   Mr Claymore's ward. Miss Price.

MRS MILCOTE   A pretty girl, but so thin. Is she sickening?

MRS LYNCH   I'm afraid I don't know.

Mrs Lynch moves away to continue her work.

Alexander enters, carrying some music. He glances about to make sure his father isn't watching and then makes his way up to the gallery and begins to talk to one of the Musicians.

Meshak's face appears at a window. He looks about for Melissa but he cannot see her and he disappears again.

People are dancing now as more and more guests arrive. Isobel, Melissa and Thomas enter.

Mr Claymore makes a great show of being in awe of Melissa's beauty and asks her to dance. She curtsies politely but refuses and walks away.

Miss Price sees Mrs Lynch and catches her eye. Mrs Lynch passes close to her.

MISS PRICE   Have you seen him?

MRS LYNCH   Go to the terrace.   30

Mrs Lynch walks out through the French windows onto the moonlit terrace. After a moment, Miss Price appears.

MISS PRICE   Have you seen the Coram Man? I have to know if she's all right.

MRS LYNCH   I know he's in the district. I will ask him to come to you.

MISS PRICE   Thank you. I have to know.   35

Mrs Lynch starts to go back inside.

Mrs Lynch? Is there anything you can give me … to stop me … I'm so scared that another baby will come.

MRS LYNCH	You have to stop him touching you.
MISS PRICE	How? He does what he likes. I'm dependent 40 on him.
MRS LYNCH	If you think there's the slightest chance you are with child, you must come to me immediately. There are things I can give you. Things I can try to stop the baby. You 45 understand?

Miss Price nods. Mrs Lynch goes inside. After a few moments Miss Price goes in too.

In the ballroom, Sir William is standing with Mrs Milcote. He notices Alexander talking to the Musicians.

SIR WILLIAM	Alexander! What are you doing there?
ALEXANDER	I'm sorry, Sir, I was just …
SIR WILLIAM	Let's have you out on that dance floor.
ALEXANDER	I don't like dancing. 50
MRS MILCOTE	Melissa is without a partner, look.
SIR WILLIAM	Capital. She'll do. Go and ask her.
ALEXANDER	I'd rather not.
SIR WILLIAM	Nonsense. Half the men in this room would rather not but we just have to get on with it. 55 Go on, boy.

Alexander strides over to Melissa, his jaw set with irritation. She is standing alone.

ALEXANDER	Will you dance with me?
MELISSA	With you?

She glances round and sees her mother's expectant face.

I'll dance with you if you say please.

Alexander looks very surprised. He thinks for a moment, then says:

ALEXANDER   Please.   60

MELISSA   Very well. Thank you.

She takes his hand and he leads her onto the floor. Her heart is pounding. This is the first time she has danced in public before. As they take up a position and wait for the beat, she smiles at him nervously. And then they begin to dance. Alexander is rigid and expressionless.

Isobel is now dancing with Mr Claymore. She is giggling and adoring the attention. Lady Ashbrook is watching and smiling to see Isobel so happy.

Melissa begins to realise that Alexander's heart is not in the dance. It reaches the point where he is being positively rude and making her look foolish.

If you don't like to dance, why did you ask me?

ALEXANDER   For the same reason I do everything around here; because my father told me to.

Melissa stops dancing abruptly and stares up at him, right into his eyes.

What?   65

She continues to stare. She is fighting back tears.

What?

Melissa starts to run off. He catches her arm.

Melissa?

She shakes his arm off and runs outside onto the terrace. He follows her out, looking confused.

Meshak, who has been watching them dancing from the terrace, ducks into the shadows.

What's wrong?

MELISSA   If you think I want any part in this, you're wrong!   70

ALEXANDER   What do you mean?

MELISSA   Do you think I don't hate this too? Being pushed together, being forced in front of your eyes like some prize pony!

ALEXANDER   I ...   75

MELISSA   You are not the only person in this house who feels things, you're not the only sensitive person, you're just the only one who's so wrapped up in your own feelings that you don't notice anyone else's!   80

Silence.

ALEXANDER   I'm sorry. I hadn't ... I'm very sorry. I don't want to upset you.

Pause.

MELISSA   I just wish ...

ALEXANDER   What?

MELISSA   I just wish they'd leave me alone. Trapped. It's feeling trapped into things. I hate it.   85

ALEXANDER   Yes. I really am sorry.

MELISSA   So am I.

They are quiet for a moment. The music drifts out from the house.

ALEXANDER If I asked you again, would you dance with me? Out here? We could dance just for us.

Melissa nods. Alexander approaches her.

Please. Would you please dance with me, 90 please?

Melissa laughs. She takes his hand and they begin to dance. This time it feels different. There is something between them – they both feel very aware of their bodies, of their hands touching and they look into each other's eyes.

Meshak cannot stand to see this. He suddenly collapses to the ground in a 'dead' state. Alexander and Melissa hear him fall and look to see what has happened.

MELISSA Oh. Do you think he's all right?

ALEXANDER I'm not sure.

Melissa kneels beside him and touches his forehead.

MELISSA Poor thing.

ALEXANDER I've seen him before. I think I should get help. 95

Suddenly Otis appears.

OTIS Just leave him. He'll get up in a minute.

Alexander and Melissa stand up and look at Otis, who bows.

OTIS Otis Gardiner – at your service, Master Ashbrook.

But at this moment, Thomas appears.

THOMAS There you are. The musician's master was
looking for you. He says it's time. Come on. 100

MELISSA Time for what?

ALEXANDER Come with me.

*He takes her hand and they go back inside. Otis
kicks Meshak.*

OTIS Get up, cretin!

Mrs Lynch comes outside.

MRS LYNCH You shouldn't do that.

She crosses to Meshak and watches him.

I saw something like it once. A young 105
gentleman in France. He didn't live long.

OTIS He'll live to a ripe old age, just you watch. I
should have drowned him at birth.

MRS LYNCH But you didn't.

OTIS Maybe it's true what they say – blood's 110
thicker than water.

*Meshak comes out of his 'dead' state and gets to
his feet, shakily.*

MESHAK Angel loves Meshak.

OTIS You and your angels. There ain't no angels!

*Meshak runs off, distressed. At the same time,
Miss Price comes onto the terrace.*

MISS PRICE You found him …

*But Mr Claymore appears in the doorway behind
her. Miss Price looks at him in alarm.*

CLAYMORE   What are you doing out here? Come back   115
inside.

*Miss Price goes back in. Mr Claymore looks at Otis
and at Mrs Lynch.*

MRS LYNCH   Good evening, Sir.

*They stare at each other for a few moments, then
he goes back inside.*

*In the ballroom the Musicians come to the end of a
song. Alexander stands up in the gallery and
addresses the guests.*

ALEXANDER   Ladies and gentlemen.

*The Guests look up in surprise. Thomas beams up
at him. Melissa watches anxiously. Sir William is
standing with Lady Ashbrook. He frowns.*

SIR WILLIAM   What on earth … ?

ALEXANDER   As you all know, it is my mother's birthday   120
tomorrow.

A ripple of applause goes round the room.

As a surprise for her, I would like to sing for
her. I would like to sing a song which I have
written and arranged myself.

*The Guests make impressed and appreciative
noises. Sir William is rigid with anger. He is about
to step forward and speak. Lady Ashbrook puts a
hand on his arm.*

LADY ASHBROOK   *(quietly)* Don't. Please.   125

The Musicians begin to play and Alexander begins to sing – 'I Will Praise Thee'. His voice and the music are so beautiful that tears come to eyes and mouths fall open. Melissa steps forward – closer and closer to him.

ALEXANDER I will praise thee, praise thee, O Lord,
With my whole heart,
I'll praise, praise, praise thee, O Lord,
I will praise thee, I will praise thee,
I will praise thee with my whole heart.   130
I shall show forth all thy marvellous works,
I will be glad and rejoice in thee,
And rejoice, rejoice,
I'll be glad and rejoice in thee …

He nears the end of the song. But suddenly his voice gives way. He tries to keep singing but it happens again. He tries again, but the sound he makes is low and rough.

The Musicians are not sure what to do. Gradually they stop playing. He tries one more time. It is no use. He stares down at his feet, breathing hard. There is silence for a moment.

LADY ASHBROOK *(going to him)* That was beautiful.   135

SIR WILLIAM Excellent, Alexander. I never heard you sing so well. Ladies and gentleman, it seems we have another cause to celebrate.

A round of applause goes up. Alexander looks at his father, who smiles triumphantly.

Scene 21

*Sir William and Lady Ashbrook are in the **drawing room** when Alexander rushes up to them.*

ALEXANDER	What's happening?
LADY ASHBROOK	Let's go and sit down, Alexander …
ALEXANDER	Was that Thomas? Was Thomas in that carriage?
SIR WILLIAM	Gone back to Gloucester. Your timing was excellent. Saved yourself the journey.
LADY ASHBROOK	Alex …
ALEXANDER	You can't do this! Why didn't you let me say goodbye?
LADY ASHBROOK	Because we knew you would get upset.
ALEXANDER	You can't do this! I want to go back.

Isobel and Melissa appear and watch with alarm.

SIR WILLIAM	Well, you can't.
ALEXANDER	I have to! I have music I want to …
SIR WILLIAM	No! My God, I wish I'd never let you near the place! Now you and I have four years of catching up to do, so get into your riding gear. You'll ride with me to inspect the mill.
ALEXANDER	No.
SIR WILLIAM	I beg your pardon?
LADY ASHBROOK	Alex …
ALEXANDER	I have work to do on my music.

Sir William slaps his face. Alexander stares at him, struggling to control himself. Then he goes to step past him but Sir William stands in his way.

Get out of my way.

SIR WILLIAM How dare you?

ALEXANDER Well I do! I do dare!

He pushes past Sir William who immediately charges after him.

LADY ASHBROOK William, no! 25

Alexander storms into the drawing room and sits down at the harpsichord. He begins to play but Sir William appears beside him and brings the lid crashing down. Alexander just manages to pull his fingers free in time. He stares at his father in anger and disbelief.

SIR WILLIAM Get it out of here! Mrs Lynch! Mrs Lynch! I want this out! And all the rest, out!

Mrs Lynch comes hurrying up.

I want every musical instrument out of this house!

LADY ASHBROOK William, please ... 30

SIR WILLIAM Every last one!

ALEXANDER No!

SIR WILLIAM Every pipe, every fiddle, every drum, every blasted one!

MRS LYNCH Yes, Sir. 35

Alexander gets up suddenly and strides out of the room.

ISOBEL Alex? Alex?

But he walks past her as if she isn' t there.

Scene 22

*We are plunged into Alexander's head – full of
music and colours and memories of raised voices
crashing in, then fading away. He hears himself
singing in his clear treble voice. He is desperate
and angry. It rises to fever pitch before he
collapses face down on his bed, exhausted and
wretched.*

Night. Melissa comes silently to the door of
Alexander's bedroom.

MELISSA   *(whispering)* Alexander?

He doesn' t reply.

Alexander, it's Melissa.

He looks round at her.

Can I talk to you?

Pause.

ALEXANDER   Yes.

She crosses to his bed and sits down.

MELISSA   It's the cruellest thing I've ever known.   5

ALEXANDER   I'm going out of my mind. I swear it. I swear
I will go mad. I don't know what I am
without music. I don't know why to move.
Why to breathe.

Pause.

MELISSA   Come with me.   10

ALEXANDER   What?

MELISSA	I want you to come with me. Trust me.
ALEXANDER	Where are we going?
MELISSA	To Waterside. Be very quiet. Mrs Lynch hears everything. 15

Scene 23

Waterside. Melissa and Alexander enter. Melissa's candle throws shadowy light around the room. She walks to a corner and pulls away a sheet to reveal the old virginals. Alexander gasps. He hurries towards it.

MELISSA   I hid it.

Alexander is overwhelmed.

I know it isn't much, and it's out of tune …

ALEXANDER   It's enough. It's enough.

MELISSA   If we keep it in this corner, I don't think the children will take any notice of it. And as long   5 as you only come here at night …

ALEXANDER   I don't know how to thank you.

MELISSA   Just play something.

Alexander plays. Melissa watches, thrilled that he is happy.

ALEXANDER   I can stand anything … I can stand mills and   10 ships and harvests as long as I can do this.

MELISSA   And I'll make sure you have paper and ink and anything you need for your work.

ALEXANDER   I'll come here every single night.

MELISSA   Yes.   15

He stares at her.

ALEXANDER You've saved me.

MELISSA I couldn't bear to see you unhappy.

ALEXANDER You're wonderful.

He kisses her, tentatively at first but she kisses him back and soon they are kissing passionately.

At the window, Meshak's face appears, white and shocked.

Alexander draws Melissa out of Waterside and into the woods. In the darkness, he takes her in his arms and covers her in kisses as they sink to the floor.

Meshak has followed them and watches until he can bear it no longer. His rage and hurt cannot be contained. For a moment we fear for Melissa and Alexander, but then he rushes back to Waterside. He charges up to the virginals and smashes it to pieces.

MESHAK My angel!

Scene 24

*The same night. Otis is camped in the **woods** near the cottage, beside a dark, stagnant lake. Mrs Lynch arrives and looks about for him. Otis creeps up behind her and covers her eyes.*

OTIS Who's this sneaking into my lair?

MRS LYNCH Let go of me, Otis.

He does so, and kisses her, clumsily.

OTIS Ready to go, my lady?

MRS LYNCH You've been drinking.

| OTIS | Yes I have. Drinking and thinking and laying down plans for you and me. | 5 |

MRS LYNCH I've only come to say goodbye.

OTIS But you're coming with me.

MRS LYNCH I'm not.

OTIS Yes you are. You're coming with me to make our fortunes from Mr Coram. The wonderful 10 Mr Coram. There are two more ladies asking for the Coram Man. One of 'em's in Bristol. Bristol! News travels fast, eh? Come with me. We'll put our money in a ship – invest. There's tidy profits to be made … 15

MRS LYNCH Forget it.

OTIS We'd be unstoppable – you and me.

MRS LYNCH I don't throw in my lot with anyone. I learnt that a long time ago.

Pause.

OTIS Fine. Fine. I'll go on my own. I'm not going 20 to spend the rest of my life grovelling around for scraps even if you are.

MRS LYNCH I'll get word to you if there's anything for you here.

OTIS Sometimes I wonder if you want to get out of 25 here at all. Maybe you've found your place.

MRS LYNCH If I stay in that house it's because I choose to stay. Because it suits me to stay. When I go, and I will go, it'll be because I'm ready. I'm not going to gamble with my future. For you 30 or anyone.

She starts to walk away. He grabs her and kisses her. She kisses him back.

OTIS	Stay the night. Come on. Stay the night.
MRS LYNCH	I couldn't sleep in these woods.
OTIS	You wouldn't have to sleep.
MRS LYNCH	I have to be up before dawn. 35
OTIS	The highly efficient Mrs Lynch. The oh-so-trustworthy Mrs Lynch. You know all the tricks, don't you? Keep a man keen. Where did you learn all your tricks, eh?
MRS LYNCH	I don't use tricks with you, Otis. If I did, you 40 wouldn't stand a chance.

He suddenly laughs.

I'll see you next time. Yes?

OTIS	Yes.
MRS LYNCH	And remember what I said – be careful.

She leaves. He watches her go, smiling.

Scene 25

*Two days later. Morning. The whole of **Ashbrook House** is filled with Lady Ashbrook's cry.*

LADY ASHBROOK	Alex! Alex! No!

Sir William bursts from the drawing room into the hallway with a letter in his hand. Mrs Milcote and Isobel come hurrying to him. Melissa follows. Mrs Lynch also appears.

No!

MRS MILCOTE	What is it, Sir William? What has happened?
SIR WILLIAM	It's Alexander. He's gone.

On hearing this, Melissa rushes away. She runs to Waterside.

ISOBEL   Gone?

5

SIR WILLIAM   Go to her, will you?

Mrs Milcote and Isobel rush into the drawing room.

(To Mrs Lynch) Tell the grooms to saddle the horses.

Sir William hurries off.

Scene 26

*At **Waterside**, Melissa walks in and sees the broken virginals. She is horrified. Next to it she sees a note. She rushes to it and picks it up. It has her name on it. She opens it with trembling hands and reads it.*

MELISSA   God keep you, Alexander.

Scene 27

*Several weeks later. Melissa, Isobel, Edward and Alice are at **Waterside**. All the old excitement and joy about the place has gone. Isobel is playing a game with Edward and Alice using the dolls, but their hearts aren't in it. Melissa is detached.*

ISOBEL   Well, come on. It seems like I'm the only one playing. Alice, you have to make her go to the palace.

ALICE   She said she didn't want to go to the palace.

ISOBEL   Well, she does now. What's your man called,   5
           Edward?

EDWARD   He hasn't got a name.

ISOBEL   Of course he has a name.

EDWARD   Alexander. He's called Alexander.

           The mention of the name draws everyone up short.

ISOBEL   Think of another name.   10

EDWARD   No. He's Alexander.

           Alice starts to cry.

ISOBEL   Now look what you've done.

           Melissa goes to Alice.

MELISSA   Don't get upset. Wherever he is, I'm sure
           Alex is thinking of you.

ISOBEL   No he's not. He's not thinking of us at all. If   15
           he was thinking of us he wouldn't have
           stayed away for weeks and weeks without
           telling us where he is.

MELISSA   I expect he feels he has no choice.

EDWARD   Papa will flog him when he finds him.   20

ISOBEL   It's mean and selfish and he's ruined
           everything!

           Melissa starts to go.

ISOBEL   Where are you going?

MELISSA   I'm sorry. I have to … I have to be alone for
           a while.   25

ISOBEL   That's all you ever say now! Why do you
          have to be so miserable? He's not your
          brother.

          *Melissa leaves. She gets as far away from
          Waterside as she can before she has to stop to
          vomit against a tree. She is feeling terrible –
          physically and emotionally.*

Scene 28

*In the **drawing room** at Ashbrook House. The
family are gathered around Sir William. In front of
Sir William there is a desk, on which there is a
large bible, a pen and some ink. The mood is
sombre.*

SIR WILLIAM   As you are all aware, it is now six months
               since Alexander saw fit to leave us. And as
               you are also aware, despite my best efforts,
               I have been unable to find him.

               *Isobel sobs. Lady Ashbrook looks down, trying to
               control herself.*

               I can no longer spend my time, nor tie up the   5
               valuable resources of this estate in looking
               for him. It is quite clear that he does not
               intend to be found. I have therefore reached
               a decision. This is our family bible. In it are
               written the names of the Ashbrooks going   10
               back for generations.

               *He picks up the pen, and crosses out Alexander's
               name.*

From this day onwards, Alexander does not exist. Edward, you will become the next Lord Ashbrook and I have no doubt that you will be worthy of the title. I never wish to hear mention of Alexander again. 15

ISOBEL Mama? *(Lady Ashbrook will not look at her)* You can't do this!

SIR WILLIAM It is done.

Isobel leaves the room in tears. Mrs Milcote, Melissa and the children follow her out. Lady Ashbrook is sitting very still.

LADY ASHBROOK I have never wavered in my devotion to you. And I have wholeheartedly supported 20 you in everything you do. But it is duty alone now which stops me from speaking out against this. It is wrong. I bore him. He is a part of me. And of you. Nothing can ever change that. 25

She leaves. Sir William stares down at the bible.

Scene 29

*In her bed at **Ashbrook House**, Melissa is tossing and turning, disturbed by dreams. She dreams she sees Alexander coming towards her, holding a lantern.*

His face is bright and smiling. But down around his feet there are babies. A baby crawls up onto Melissa's bed. She screams with shock and wakens. She is trembling. She just sits for a moment, trying to steady her heart. She takes stock of her dream. There is an agonising thought growing in her mind. She gets out of bed and crosses to a mirror. She looks down at her stomach, and runs her hands over it. It is growing. She keeps her hand on it and stares at her reflection.

Outside the door of her room, Mrs Lynch appears and looks in at Melissa. Melissa sees her.

MRS LYNCH Do you want my help?

Melissa stares at her.

You will need it. Tell me when you need it.

Mrs Lynch goes. Melissa is breathing hard. She turns to the bed and grabs a blanket and wraps it around herself to cover the bump. She looks in the mirror to see if it can be concealed. She sinks to her knees and weeps.

MELISSA Alexander …

Scene 30

Several months later. In the house, Isobel rushes up to Mrs Lynch. She is white-faced and shaking.

ISOBEL Mrs Lynch?

MRS LYNCH Is it Melissa?

ISOBEL *(nodding)* She's at Waterside. She wants you. She's screaming with pain. I think she's dying.

MRS LYNCH She's not dying. Her baby is coming.   5

ISOBEL   Baby? What are you talking about?

MRS LYNCH   Melissa is having your brother's baby.

ISOBEL   You're lying.

MRS LYNCH   She is having Alexander's baby. It's the truth.

Isobel, through sheer shock, hits Mrs Lynch across the face. Mrs Lynch does not flinch. Isobel clasps her hand over her mouth – horrified at what she has done and what is happening.

You must be very calm now. You must go   10
back and help her while I fetch her mother
and bring the things we need.

ISOBEL   No. She said not her mother. She said not to
tell her mother.

MRS LYNCH   She must be told. If anything were to go wrong   15
… it's only right that she should be there.

ISOBEL   What will go wrong?

MRS LYNCH   Calm yourself. Go back to her. And tell no
one of this. No one.

Scene 31

*At **Waterside**, Melissa is on the ground, struggling with the pain of a contraction. Meshak appears in the open doorway and stares at her, horrified to see her like this. She sees him and her eyes meet his.*

MELISSA   The baby …

He darts away, as Isobel comes rushing in and goes straight to Melissa. Isobel is struggling to take in the situation.

ISOBEL   Why didn't you tell me?

MELISSA   Is she coming?

ISOBEL   Yes. Why didn't you tell me?

MELISSA   I didn't want it to be true.   5

ISOBEL   Alexander's baby.

MELISSA   Oh, hold my hand.

*She screams in agony. Outside the window,
Meshak closes his ears.*

*Mrs Lynch, half-supporting Mrs Milcote, arrives in
front of the cottage.*

MRS MILCOTE   Here?

MRS LYNCH   Yes.

MRS MILCOTE   Lord help me, this can't be happening.   10

MRS LYNCH   Remember, she must not be allowed to hold
the baby. She must not become attached to it.

MRS MILCOTE   She can't keep it. Oh, my Lord, what will
become of us?

MRS LYNCH   No, she can't keep it. Are we agreed that we   15
will give it to the Coram Man? Look at me. We
will give it to the Coram Man?

MRS MILCOTE   Yes. The Coram Man. But … but how will he
know to come?

MRS LYNCH   He is already here.   20

*They go into the cottage. Melissa's baby is
coming. Mrs Milcote rushes to her side.*

MELISSA   I'm sorry. I'm sorry.

*Mrs Milcote kisses her face and hands. Mrs Lynch
delivers the baby. Isobel is crying with shock and*

joy. Mrs Lynch hands the baby to Isobel while she cuts the umbilical cord. The baby is still and silent. Isobel is overwhelmed with wonder and love.

ISOBEL   Look. Oh, look, Melissa. Look.

Melissa holds out her arms to take her son. But Mrs Lynch takes him quickly from Isobel. Mrs Milcote takes off her pink shawl and hands it to Mrs Lynch.

MRS MILCOTE   Here …

Mrs Lynch wraps the shawl around the baby and walks out of the cottage. Mrs Milcote rushes after her.

Wait!

Mrs Lynch pauses. Mrs Milcote takes the baby from her and cradles it in her arms.

My grandson. God bless you. God bless you.   25

She kisses his head. Mrs Lynch takes him back.

MRS LYNCH   Tell her it was dead.

Mrs Milcote looks aghast.

It's the only way. Tell her.

Mrs Lynch rushes off along the path to the lake. Meshak comes out from his hiding place to follow her. He comes face to face with Mrs Milcote and they both freeze like frightened animals. Then Meshak runs off after Mrs Lynch.

He arrives at the lake in time to see her handing the baby to Otis.

Come to me soon. I'll have the money for you.

OTIS Tonight?

*She nods and then rushes back to the cottage.
Meshak approaches Otis cautiously, staring at the
baby – his angel's baby. Otis sees him.*

Here. Bury it with the rest. It's dead anyway. 30

*Meshak takes the baby slowly, hardly believing he
can hold it in his hands. Otis thrusts a spade at him.*

Get on with it, you worthless idiot!

*Meshak stares at his father. All he can see in his
eyes are hatred and contempt. He takes the baby
to the lake. He stares at the baby's face.*

MESHAK Angel child. Angel child. Wake up. Wake up.

*He throws aside the pink shawl, now stained with
blood. Gently, he lowers the baby into the water.
He takes water in his fingers and sprinkles it on
the baby's head.*

Wake up.

Suddenly the baby lets out a cry.

Shh, shh. Shh, shh. Mustn't let Da hear.

*He puts his finger to the baby's mouth and it
stops crying. Meshak looks round towards Otis –
he is not watching him.*

Angel child. Come with Meshak. Safe with 35
Meshak.

*He tucks the baby under his jacket and stumbles
off into the woods.*

Scene 32

The following scene takes place under music, so that the words are not heard and only the action tells the story.

*In the **woods**, beside the stagnant lake, the pink shawl blows in the wind. Day turns to night, and night to day. Alice and Edward come running through the woods in winter sunshine. They have found some small skulls and stuck them on the end of sticks. They are chasing each other with them.*

Mrs Milcote comes along after them and sees what they are playing with. Horrified, she takes the skulls off them. Alice points to where they found them – near to the water. Mrs Milcote sends the children back to the house. Slowly, she approaches the spot which Alice pointed to and crouches down. There are more bones. She stands and backs away. Then she sees the shawl. It is lying in mud nearby. She picks it up and sees the blood on it. She doubles over with shock and grief. Then she hurriedly bundles it up and tucks it inside her coat. She rushes back to the house.

Scene 33

*Men with dogs are digging up the ground by the **lake**. Mr Claymore is directing them. Sir William and Lady Ashbrook arrive. Two Men pass by them, carefully carrying cloths containing human remains.*

CLAYMORE *(to the Men)* Take them to the church and lay them out beside the others. *(Addressing the Ashbrooks)* My Lord. Lady Ashbrook.

SIR WILLIAM	You've found more then?
CLAYMORE	That's nine so far.	5

LADY ASHBROOK	It's too horrible. On our own land.
SIR WILLIAM	But you have someone?
CLAYMORE	We've apprehended a fellow called Otis Gardiner. A tinker. He's known to camp in these woods. Two local women have come forward to say they paid him to take their babies from them.	10

LADY ASHBROOK	Paid him?
CLAYMORE	He was supposed to take them somewhere safe.	15

SIR WILLIAM	For God's sake.
LADY ASHBROOK	Those poor women.
SIR WILLIAM	Has he confessed? This tinker?
CLAYMORE	Not yet. But if the evidence against him continues to mount, I'll hang him anyway – confession or no confession.	20

Scene 34

*In the **local court room**, Otis is in the dock. Mr Claymore is presiding. The room and the gallery are packed with People. Amongst them are Sir William and Lady Ashbrook.*

Mrs Lynch is also there, sitting quietly to one side, watching. The room is in uproar – people are shouting and shaking their fists and throwing things at Otis. Otis is sneering.

CLAYMORE	Silence! Silence!

The room quietens.

Otis Gardiner, you have been found guilty on three counts of murder. Only our Lord God can know how many other heinous acts you have committed in the name of greed and cruelty. 5

There is another outbreak of shouting. The following lines rise above the music:

Silence! Otis Gardiner, it is my duty to sentence you to death by hanging! Take him to the gaol.

OTIS What about them as gave me the brats? Why 10 aren't they guilty? Out of sight, out of mind, eh? Pay me to do their dirty work!

Otis is dragged away with the Crowd jeering and screaming at him as he goes. Mr Claymore stands and goes out of a door at the back of the room. Mrs Lynch stands up and follows him out. She is clearly going to speak to him.

Scene 35

Otis, blind-folded and gagged, is led to the gibbet. A Hangman places a noose around his neck. And he is hanged.

Act Two

Scene 1

*1750. The **Coram Foundling Hospital.** The Coram
Children are singing the Coram Hymn.*

CHILDREN   Left on the world's bleak waste forlorn,
In sin conceived, to sorrow born,
By guilt and shame fordoomed to share
No mother's love, no father's care,
No guide the devious maze to tread,   5
Above no friendly shelter spread.

*Two boys – one black, Toby, and one white, Aaron
– break away from the other Children and peer into
a very large, imposing room. At one end of the
room there is a group of anxious and desperate-
looking Mothers holding babies. At the other end
of the room there is a group of wealthy Ladies and
Gentlemen who are watching the proceedings with
interest. In the middle of the room there is a desk,
behind which a Governor sits, with a Lady to each
side of him. On the desk there is a basket covered
with a cloth. The two Ladies have pens and paper
before them.*

GOVERNOR   *(addressing the Mothers)* Those of you who
draw a white ball from the basket have been
successful. Your infants will undergo a
medical examination and, if deemed fit, will   10
enter the Coram Hospital.

Those of you who draw a red ball must await
the outcome of those said examinations to
see if a place becomes available once more.

Those of you who draw a black ball have   15
been unsuccessful and you must take your
infants away. Today we are offering three
places. May God be with you all.

LADY   *(nodding to a Mother)* Step forward, please.

*The mother approaches the desk. She puts her
hand under the cloth into the basket and draws
out a ball. It is red. One of the Ladies records this.*

GOVERNOR   Step to the side please, Miss.   20

*She does so. The Lady nods to the next mother
who comes forward. She draws a ball from the
basket. It is black. A sympathetic noise comes
from the wealthy Ladies.*

MOTHER   No. Let me try again. Please. I'll come back
tomorrow.

LADY   The pressure of numbers does not permit that.

MOTHER   He's a lovely boy. He's healthy and beautiful.

LADY   Step aside please, Miss.   25

MOTHER   This isn't fair!

GOVERNOR   It is the fairest system we could possibly
employ. You all have an equal chance.

LADY   Step aside please, Miss.

*Mrs Hendry, the Matron of the Hospital enters and
sees the Boys spying on them.*

MRS HENDRY   Aaron! Toby! Get away from there at once!   30
You know you shouldn't be there.

TOBY AND AARON   Sorry, Mrs Hendry. Sorry, Ma'am.

They run off.

Scene 2

*Toby and Aaron come charging **outside** into the fresh air.*

TOBY If I'm a black ball and you're a white ball, where are all the red balls?

Aaron laughs.

AARON Mish can be a red ball. He's a carrot-top.

TOBY Yes! Mish is a red ball.

A group of girls suddenly runs up and surrounds Aaron. They begin chanting:

GIRLS Quick, quick, say your prayers,   5
Blow out the candle and climb the stairs,
Who will come to kiss you goodnight,
Close your eyes and shut them tight,
In and out and round and round,
Lie down, stay on the ground,   10
In and out and round and round,
She's creeping up without a sound,
It could be her, it could be me,
But which one will it be,
In and out and round and round,   15
Don't move, stay on the ground,
In and out and round and round,
Open your eyes 'cause you've been found!

Aaron is kissed by a cheeky girl – Molly Jenkins. Toby laughs his head off.

AARON Get off, Molly Jenkins.

The Girls laugh and run off.

TOBY	She loves you. She wants your babies.	20
AARON	No one wants babies!	

Mrs Hendry appears. She rings a bell. Lots of Children run up and form two lines – Boys on one side and Girls on the other. Toby and Aaron join their line.

MRS HENDRY John, Peter – stables!
Jane, Constance – dairy!
Stephen, Joseph – wood-shed!
Mary, Charlotte – wash-room! 25
Alfred, Samuel – cow-shed!
Anne, Molly – kitchens!

Aaron, Toby …

TOBY *AND* **AARON** *(quietly)* Garden. Garden. Garden …

MRS HENDRY Garden! 30

TOBY *AND* **AARON** Yes!

They tear off to the gardens.

TOBY Let's find him!

AARON Mish! Mish!

They spot Mish standing like a scarecrow in the vegetable garden, waving his arms to shoo away the birds. It is Meshak Gardiner, so much healthier and happier looking that he is almost unrecognisable.

TOBY There!

AARON Mish! 35

They rush to him and fling their arms around him. He is thrilled to see them and picks them up and spins them round.

MISH	Angel child! Tobykins!
AARON	Was I a white ball or a red ball, Mish?
MISH	No balls in the vegetables. Not allowed.
AARON	No. When you brought me here?
TOBY	I didn't need a ball because I was special. My 40 mother was a princess in Africa. And we'll go and find her and she'll look after all of us.
AARON	On a big ship.
TOBY *AND* MISH	Across the dark ocean.
AARON	Was I a white ball, Mish, when you brought 45 me here?
MISH	*(confused)* No balls. They were kind to Mish and his Angel child.
TOBY	He means they didn't have the balls then. They just let anyone in. 50
AARON	That's why they let you in.

Toby growls and tries to squash Aaron's head.

TOBY	*(to Mish)* Are you his Da?
MISH	Yes.
TOBY	Are you his Ma?
MISH	Yes. Mish Da and Mish Ma. 55

The Boys laugh. Aaron hugs him.

AARON	You're so funny, Mish.
MISH	Apples today.
AARON	Be my horse.
TOBY	Be my horse. It's my turn.

Mish picks both of them up and carries them off.

Scene 3

*The **Chapel** at the Foundling Hospital. The organ is being played. Aaron creeps in – drawn by the wonderful, thrilling music. He sees the organist – a broad-backed man, hunched over his instrument. Every so often he breaks off and scribbles something on a piece of paper, muttering to himself. This organist, unknown to Aaron, is George Frideric Handel. Aaron creeps further forward and finds a hiding place to listen from. The music holds and transports him.*

A Cleaner enters with a bucket, making an enormous clatter. Handel stops playing immediately and turns on him.

HANDEL   Du lieber Gott.

CLEANER   Sorry, Sir. I was told the rehearsal was finished, Sir.

HANDEL   Quiet with you!

The Cleaner hurries out but, in his irritation, Handel has dropped several pages of his manuscript which flutter down to the floor.

Mein Gott!   5

Aaron scurries from his hiding place and collects them up. He takes them to Handel and gives them to him.

Thank you, my boy.

AARON   You're welcome, Sir.

Aaron turns to go.

HANDEL	Wait. What are you doing here, creeping around like a little mouse, eh?
AARON	Sorry. Sorry, Sir. I heard the music and I wanted to see.
HANDEL	You like music?
AARON	Yes, Sir. I love music.
HANDEL	Can you play?
AARON	No, Sir.
HANDEL	Sing you in the choir?
AARON	No, Sir. I'm not old enough yet, Sir.

Handel suddenly stands and picks Aaron up. He stands him on the organ stool.

HANDEL	Sing me something.
AARON	*(alarmed)* Sing?
HANDEL	Go on. Sing!

Aaron sings 'He Shall Feed His Flock'. He sings it perfectly. His voice is clear and strong and passionate. When he has finished, Handel stares at him for some time.

HANDEL	How do you know this music?
AARON	I've heard it here, Sir. When I'm in the schoolroom I can hear them practising – the choir and all the musicians.
HANDEL	Do you know what this music is?
AARON	I know it's for a concert. To raise money for us. We're orphans.
HANDEL	This music is mine. It is called *Messiah*.
AARON	Really? It's the best music I've ever heard.

10

15

20

25

| HANDEL | I should think it is. | 30 |

Handel stares at him.

You have the gift.

| AARON | *(confused)* We aren't allowed gifts. |

| HANDEL | You have the gift of music. The greatest gift. See – |

He makes Aaron look closely at his eyes.

You have made me weep. What is your name? 35

| AARON | Aaron. Aaron Dangerfield. Mr Dangerfield is my benefactor. I'll be apprenticed to him. |

| HANDEL | What to do? |

| AARON | Cabinet-maker, Sir. |

| HANDEL | Nein, nein, nein. This cannot be so. I will talk 40 to your choirmaster about you – your Mr … |

| AARON | Ledbury, Sir. |

| HANDEL | Yes. I will talk to him about you. |

A bell sounds in the yard.

Yes. Run along now.

Aaron gets down and starts to go.

| AARON | Goodbye, Sir. | 45 |

| HANDEL | I will talk to him. Aaron Dangerfield. |

Scene 4

*Mrs Hendry is in her **office**. A maid enters, leading Toby and Aaron in. They look sheepish.*

| MAID | The boys you wanted, Mrs Hendry. |

MRS HENDRY	Thank you.

The maid leaves.

AARON	Toby. Do you know why you are here?
TOBY	Is it because of the mud pie?
MRS HENDRY	No. No it isn't. Though you can tell me about 5 that later if you would like.
TOBY	No thanks, Ma'am.
MRS HENDRY	Boys, I have asked you here to tell you that your time with us is at an end. On Friday you will both be leaving to begin new lives. Toby, 10 you will go to join the household of your benefactor, Mr Gaddarn, as a liveried servant. You will be housed and fed. You will be allowed to attend church on Sundays and have one day off a year. Mr Gaddarn is a good 15 and important man. He gives a great deal of money to support our work. I trust you will serve him well.
TOBY	Yes, Ma'am.
MRS HENDRY	Aaron. You are not yet eight and normally 20 a little young to be apprenticed out. But Mr Handel believes you have superior talents in music. We have spoken with Mr Dangerfield and he has kindly agreed that you may now be apprenticed to a 25 musician named Mr Brook, a protegee of Mr Handel. You will be instructed in the art of music copying and you will also be given musical tuition.

AARON   Music! I really want to do music!   30

MRS HENDRY   Now, as you are probably aware, it is our practice when a boy leaves to give him back any token which he came here with. Many of you had mothers who loved you very dearly and wished you to have something to   35 remember them by.

She picks up a colourful string of beads from a tray on her desk.

Toby, this string of beads was around your neck when you were brought here.

Toby takes it. He is amazed and overwhelmed. His mother must have held this, touched it.

TOBY   Do you know where my mother is?

MRS HENDRY   No, I'm afraid I don't. The stranger who   40 brought you here said he found you in Bristol. It is most likely that your mother was a slave, en route to the Indies.

TOBY   But she's a princess. And she's free now.

Mrs Hendry only smiles.

MRS HENDRY   Aaron … I'm afraid we have nothing for you.   45 There was nothing with you when you came.

Aaron is deeply disappointed. He fights back tears.

As you know, it was Mish who brought you here. He was in a very sorry state himself and we could ascertain nothing about where he found you. I'm sorry.   50

TOBY   But you've got Mish. He's like your token.

MRS HENDRY   Quite right. And that's more than many
             have.

AARON   Yes.

MRS HENDRY   So, on Friday a carriage will be sent to collect   55
             you, Toby; and Aaron, Mr Ledbury himself
             will accompany you to Mr Brook's. Go forth
             bravely, boys. Be a credit to Mr Coram and to
             all of us.

Scene 5

Toby and Aaron run outside.

TOBY   I'm going in a carriage!

AARON I'm going to learn music!

TOBY   I'm going to be liveried!

AARON Liveried means covered in liver.

TOBY   No it does not!   5

       *They fight and tumble together. Then they stop
       and are quiet for a moment.*

AARON Can I see the necklace?

       *Toby takes it carefully from his pocket and lets him
       take it for a moment.*

TOBY   Don't break it.

AARON Do you think she made it?

TOBY   Course she did.

AARON I like the colours.   10

       *Toby takes it back. Aaron watches him staring at it
       and feeling the beads between his fingers.*

We will still be friends, won't we?

TOBY Course. We'll always be friends.

Aaron goes to find Mish in the garden. He is suddenly feeling very sad. Mish stops what he is doing and hugs him tightly. Aaron starts to cry.

MISH Angel child has to go. I know. Best. Best for Angel child. Mish will come and watch for you. Watch over you. Always there. Always there for his Angel child. 15

AARON I'll come back and see you all the time. And when I'm grown up, I'll sing and make lots of money and I'll come and get you, and you and me and Toby will go and find his mother. 20

MISH On a big ship.

AARON Across the dark ocean.

They hug some more. Mish dries Aaron's eyes.

Mish … I know you're my Ma and my Da, but did I ever have a real mother? Like Toby? I 25 mean, a lady?

Mish looks away and shakes his head.

Try to remember. Please. Did you ever see her? A lady? Did she speak to you? Was she beautiful?

MISH Mish Da, Mish Ma. 30

Aaron nods, resignedly.

AARON I love you, Mish.

MISH I love you, Angel child. My Angel child.

Scene 6

*Aaron is waiting nervously in a **pleasant room** with Mr Thomas Ledbury, the Coram choirmaster. Thomas looks out of a window.*

THOMAS Well, this isn't a bad old place, eh? Good view of St Martin's Lane.

AARON Yes, Sir. Have you met Mr Brook, Sir?

THOMAS No. I understand he hasn't been in England for long. But Mr Handel thinks a lot of him. 5
Bit nervous, are you?

Aaron nods.

First time out of the hospital. It's bound to seem strange. Where was your friend off to in that carriage?

AARON A house by the river. Near Billingsgate. Mr 10
Gaddarn's.

THOMAS Well, that's not too far, eh? Think of it as moving up in the world. I remember when I first went to stay in a smart house – a huge place, much bigger than this. I kept thinking 15
I was going to get lost, or walk into someone else's room by mistake.

Aaron smiles. Thomas takes a paper bag of toffees from his pocket.

Do you want a toffee?

AARON *(excited)* Thank you, Sir.

THOMAS Oh – perhaps you'd better not eat it now if 20
you're going to sing. Put it in your pocket for later. In fact, take the lot.

AARON *(taking them)* Thanks, Mr Ledbury.

THOMAS Never know when you'll need the toffee cure. Why don't I sing you a funny song? Eh? While   25 we're waiting. Take your mind off things.

AARON Yes, please.

THOMAS Just don't tell Mrs Hendry when you see her.

Thomas crosses to a harpsichord and opens the lid.

Now then – *(Beginning to play and sing)* In   30 Gloucester Docks, so I … *(Stopping)* Perhaps not.

He sings a funny version of the Coram Hymn. Aaron giggles. Alexander enters quietly and stands in the doorway, watching. A smile breaks through his habitually sad expression.

ALEXANDER I thought I told you not to sing those songs, Thomas.

Thomas looks round in astonishment. He rises to his feet.

THOMAS Alex? Alex!   35

He flies at Alexander and they hug.

Alex. But … Edward Brook! Why didn't I think of it? Did you know it was me? I mean, did you …

ALEXANDER I hoped it was you, when Mr Handel mentioned your name.   40

THOMAS	This is wonderful. This is the best. Aaron. Sorry. This is Mr … ?
ALEXANDER	Brook.
THOMAS	Brook. Mr Brook. We knew each other when we were boys.

45

ALEXANDER	Hello, Aaron.

Alexander offers his hand to Aaron. He takes it and shakes it sombrely.

AARON	Hello, Sir.
ALEXANDER	You're very welcome here. I'm looking forward to working with you.
THOMAS	Perhaps we should … ?

50

ALEXANDER	Yes.
THOMAS	Aaron, will you sing for Mr Brook now?
ALEXANDER	Yes. Let me hear this voice I've heard so much about. And then you can go and get settled in. You must be tired.

55

AARON	Thank you, Sir.

Thomas sits at the harpsichord again. He begins to play Alexander's song – 'I Will Praise Thee'. Alexander's eyes fill with tears. Aaron finishes. Thomas looks at Alexander and smiles kindly.

THOMAS	You know me – I only have to hear something once.

Scene 7

*At **Mr Gaddarn's house**, Toby is being dressed in his 'livery'. It is the costume of an exotic African prince, with satin pantaloons and a richly embroidered jacket. On his feet he wears gorgeous, jewelled slippers which turn up at the ends, and on his head is placed a silk turban with a huge shining glass ruby in the centre of it. Finally, a silver tray is placed upon his upturned hand. Toby is in awe of this splendid costume.*

A man enters. He is wearing a powdered wig and clothes of the finest quality. This is Mr Philip Gaddarn.

GADDARN   Well. Let's have a look at you.

He looks Toby over and smiles.

Good. Very good. Do you know who I am?

TOBY   Mr Gaddarn, Sir. I'm very grateful to you, Sir.

GADDARN   And what do they call you?

TOBY   Toby. Toby Gaddarn, Sir.   5

GADDARN   Toby Gaddarn. My own little foundling boy. And what do you think of your costume? Quite the little prince, eh?

TOBY   I love it, Sir. I love this big jewel.

Pause. Mr Gaddarn is just staring at Toby.

GADDARN   So you think you'll be happy here?   10

TOBY   Oh yes, Sir.

GADDARN   Why aren't you smiling then?

Toby immediately smiles.

Is that the biggest smile you've got?

Toby smiles more broadly.

Wider.

Toby forces his mouth into an exaggerated smile.

That's how wide I expect your smile to be,   15
every time I look at you.

TOBY   Yes, Sir.

GADDARN   People like your smile. They like how black
your skin is from your head to your toes.   20

He gets very close to Toby, who keeps trying to smile.

You serve my guests. You get them anything
they want, give them anything they want. You
never say no, and you never, ever tell a soul
about anything you see in this house. Is that
understood?   25

TOBY   Yes, Sir.

GADDARN   Do you know what I do to telltales? I cut
out their tongues and nail them to their
bedposts as a reminder of what they
shouldn't have done. I'd hate to do that to   30
you. Now get out there and serve. And
smile, Toby Gaddarn.

Scene 8

*In **Alexander's house**, Alexander and Thomas are having a drink together.*

ALEXANDER Are you in touch with them?

THOMAS The occasional letter from Isobel. They're all fine and well – as far as I know.

ALEXANDER Good. That's very good.

THOMAS You've had no contact at all? 5

ALEXANDER None. Melissa – is she still with them?

THOMAS I believe so. Yes – Isobel mentioned that she and her mother are running an orphanage now, on the estate.

Alexander nods. This is affecting him very deeply.

And I hear Edward is at Eton. 10

ALEXANDER The next Lord Ashbrook. Yes, I heard.

THOMAS They did search for you, you know?

ALEXANDER Yes.

THOMAS Where did you go?

ALEXANDER Switzerland. For a while. Lied about my age 15
and got a job as a music tutor. Then I made my way to Germany …

THOMAS On the trail of Mr Handel.

ALEXANDER Yes. And that led me back here to London. I'd made some good contacts in Leipzig. 20
They'd given me letters of introduction.

THOMAS And now you're working with him. It's really extraordinary. When I think how you idolised him.

ALEXANDER	He's been very kind to me.	25
THOMAS	And your music? You must have written some wonderful stuff.	
ALEXANDER	What about you? Let me guess – you're married with three children.	
THOMAS	Not yet. But there's plenty of time for that.	30
ALEXANDER	And the Coram choir – that's really something.	
THOMAS	I love it.	
ALEXANDER	You deserve to be happy, Thomas.	
THOMAS	So do you.	35
ALEXANDER	I don't know … I don't know if I understand happiness.	
THOMAS	Of course you do.	
ALEXANDER	Even Mr Handel has noticed it. In my music. 'It's good, Alexander, very clever – but where is the joy?' That song of mine – just listening to it then – it's the best thing I've ever written.	40

Thomas is shocked and unsure whether he is serious.

I used to write for God. Everything was very clear. But since I left … *(He trails off)*

THOMAS	But your gift is still there. Of course it is.	45
ALEXANDER	No. My 'gift' is somewhere at Ashbrook.	

Pause.

I need to go back, Thomas.

Scene 9

*In the **drawing room** at Mr Gaddarn's house.*
Aaron and five other Boys are singing 'He Shall
Feed His Flock'. Handel is accompanying them on
a harpsichord. Alexander is turning the pages for
him. Thomas is conducting the Boys.

There is an audience of wealthy-looking People.
To one side, Toby is standing, dressed in his livery,
trying to smile. At the back, looking on, is Mr
Gaddarn. The piece comes to an end. The
Audience applaud. Handel takes a bow. Mr
Gaddarn comes forward.

GADDARN   I would like to begin by thanking Mr Handel
          for choosing to hold this – the first of what
          he terms his 'rehearsals' – in my humble
          abode. As you are probably all aware, the
          music these fine little fellows have sung for   5
          us today is by way of an appetiser for the
          performance of Mr Handel's masterwork …

HANDEL   *Messiah.*

          There is a ripple of applause.

GADDARN   *Messiah*, which is to take place at the Coram
          Hospital on Christmas Eve. And I'm sure you
          all agree, if this 'rehearsal' is anything to go   10
          by, then we are in for a rare and sumptuous
          treat. Mr Handel is a fellow benefactor of the
          Coram Hospital. All the money raised from
          that performance will be donated to Coram
          funds – a very generous gesture, if I might   15
          say. And what better cause could there be?
          Every time I look at my own little Coram boy,

here … *(He indicates Toby)* my heart swells
with pride. The way a nation treats its poor
and unfortunate citizens, most especially its   20
children, is a mark of how civilised it truly is.
And I say, looking about me this afternoon,
England is civilised indeed!

Everyone applauds.

Now please feel free to linger for a while, and
enjoy a little of my simple hospitality.   25

*The Audience stand and disperse. Many gather
around Handel to congratulate him. Some talk to
the Boys, some to Thomas. Mr Gaddarn passes
close to Alexander and bows as Alexander moves
aside. Alexander stares after him as though he
recognises him. Aaron goes straight to Toby, who
has begun serving delicacies from his silver tray.*

AARON Tobes! You look splendid. And look at this
place. It's like a palace!

TOBY Why haven't you been to visit me?

AARON Sorry. We've been rehearsing for the concert
all the time. And when they said we were   30
coming here, I thought it would be a good
surprise for you.

TOBY I don't like surprises any more.

He walks away.

AARON Toby?

TOBY I'm not allowed to speak to people.   35

*Thomas manages to free himself from appreciative
People and hurries towards Alexander.*

THOMAS	Alexan ... Edward!
ALEXANDER	So that's Philip Gaddarn.
THOMAS	Yes.
ALEXANDER	Aaron sang beautifully.
THOMAS	He did. Listen ...

40

ALEXANDER	His voice inspires me. I mean, it actually makes me feel that I have to write.
THOMAS	I knew you two would be good for each other. But listen. I've had a letter from Isobel. She is absolutely overjoyed to know that you're back. She sent this note for you.

45

He hands the note to Alexander.

ALEXANDER	Thank you.
THOMAS	And there's more. I asked if she would approach your parents about the idea of me taking the boys to sing at Ashbrook. A small concert like this. And your mother has said yes.

50

ALEXANDER	Yes? Really?
THOMAS	Really. She's organising it all. Inviting wealthy people from the district.

55

ALEXANDER	This is wonderful. But what about my father? Has he agreed too?
THOMAS	She didn't say. But this is the beginning, Alex. They're allowing music back – they're allowing me back! Surely it can only mean they want you back too?

60

In a quiet corner of the room, Aaron catches up with Toby.

AARON	Don't walk off. What's wrong?
TOBY	As if you care.
AARON	I'm sorry I didn't come before. You could have come and seen me, you know. 65
TOBY	I'm not allowed out.
AARON	Look.

He takes the bag of toffees out of his pocket and offers them to Toby.

Mr Ledbury gave me them. I saved half for you.

TOBY	*(taking them)* Thanks.

He turns away and starts to cry.

AARON	Tobes? Are you crying? 70
TOBY	No.
AARON	What's wrong? Aren't you happy here? Tobes?
TOBY	I hate it.
AARON	But why? It's amazing.
TOBY	You don't know what it's like. 75
AARON	Look … why don't we go to your room and you can tell …
TOBY	I haven't got a room.
AARON	Where do you sleep? *(Toby doesn' t reply)* Toby. 80
TOBY	Can we go and find my mother?
AARON	What?
TOBY	I want to go soon. Tomorrow or the day after.
AARON	Tobes, I can't. We're going to all these big houses to sing. And it's the concert in a few 85

weeks. And I like it at Mr Brook's. He's kind
and he never shouts and I love the music.

TOBY   Just go away.

AARON If you're not happy you should tell Mr
       Gaddarn.   90

TOBY   He's horrible. He's going to cut my tongue out.

AARON Cut your tongue out? Don't be silly.

TOBY   You don't believe me!

AARON I ...

TOBY   I'm going to find my mother. Soon! And   95
       you're not coming. She's my mother anyway!

*He walks out of the room. Sadly, Aaron goes back
to join the other Coram Boys.*

Scene 10

*Toby enters a **dark room**. It is wood-panelled, with
long leaded windows that look out over the docks.
There is the shadowy outline of maps on the walls,
and books on high shelves. He crosses to a large
globe which stands in the corner of the room. He
squats down next to it and turns it until he finds
Africa.*

TOBY   Africa.

*With his finger, he traces a line from Africa to the
New World.*

London. The Indies.

*He takes his mother's beads out of his pocket and
rubs them between his fingers.*

I'm coming soon. I'm coming soon.

He curls up on the floor next to the map and sobs.

Back in the drawing room, left alone with the harpsichord, Alexander tentatively begins to play. In his mind's eye, he sees Melissa, glowing like an angel.

Scene 11

A few hours later. It is dark outside. Toby has fallen asleep. People are approaching the door. Toby wakes with a start as he hears Mr Gaddarn's laugh. Horrified, he looks about and spots a silk screen at the other side of the room. He darts behind it, just in time. The room lights up with dancing shadows, as Mr Gaddarn enters carrying a candelabra which he sets down on a table. There are two other Men with him. They all sit down, and Mr Gaddarn pours drinks from a decanter.

GADDARN	I can get four boys and three girls by the end of the month.
MAN 1	Only three girls? Six would make it far more worth our while. Yours too.
GADDARN	The Coram authorities keep records. Details. 5 For every child I take possession of, I have to produce written evidence of where they're going, which family they're going to, their terms of labour. I have contacts who forge documents for me, but it takes time and 10 there's no room for mistakes. Doing it for three girls is possible, six isn't.

MAN 2   I have a contact in the North Country who
         could do the same thing for you. The Coram
         people aren't likely to go checking up   15
         there.

GADDARN I only use my own people.

MAN 2   He's good. I'll vouch for him.

         Pause. Mr Gaddarn thinks for a few moments.

GADDARN Where would the girls be going?

MAN 1   Turkey. Some would go on to North Africa.   20
         We'd keep the best ones for the harems in
         Constantinople.

GADDARN Which trader do you use?

MAN 1   Abdul Fazir. We've used him every time.

         Pause.

GADDARN I'll try for six.   25

MAN 1   Good.

GADDARN At two hundred apiece.

MAN 2   Two hundred? You're not serious?

MAN 1   That's twice the going rate.

GADDARN I thought you came to me because you   30
         wanted Coram girls. That's what they cost.
         They aren't just scum you pick up off the
         streets. They're educated, free of disease and
         they're pure as the day they were born. I'll
         guarantee them, every one. But if it's too   35
         much for you, gentlemen, there's plenty of
         other people I can do business with.

         The two Men look at each other.

MAN 1	Two hundred apiece then. But if any of them prove to be unsound in mind or body, we get our money back.

40

GADDARN	If a single one proves unsound, you'll get all your money back. But if I decide, even at the last moment, that six is too many and it has to be three, then three it will be. Agreed?

45

MEN	Agreed.

GADDARN	I will not risk my reputation with Coram. It's cost me too much. Now – I think this calls for a drink, don't you?

They knock their glasses together and drink.

MAN 2	How do you do it, Gaddarn? How do you get them onto the ships without anyone noticing?

50

MAN 1	I've often wondered that.

MAN 2	And where do you keep them – until the ships are in?

GADDARN	Trade secret, gentlemen. Let's just say ... let's just say, I move heaven and earth. *(He stands)* Shall we?

55

They leave the room. After a few moments, Toby comes out from his hiding place. He is trembling and horrified by what he has heard. He hurries from the room.

Scene 12

*Aaron and five other Coram Boys have arrived outside **Ashbrook House**. They are full of excitement and gaze at the house with awe. Mish is with them. He has paused in his task of unloading their luggage and is staring at the house. A terrible feeling is creeping through him – a realisation that he has been here before and that bad things happened when he was here.*

BOY 1   *(pointing)* That's my room!

BOY 2   I'm getting a whole wing!

Aaron goes to Mish.

AARON   It's enormous, isn't it? What's wrong?

MISH   Not here.

AARON   But this is Ashbrook House. This is where   5
we're singing.

MISH   Ashbrook.

AARON   Yes.

MISH   I'm not happy.

AARON   But why? We'll have a wonderful time.   10

MISH   I'm not happy here.

Mish runs off towards the stables.

AARON   Mish! Mish!

Thomas enters, accompanied by Lady Ashbrook, Isobel and Melissa.

THOMAS   Come on, now, boys – help with the boxes!

THOMAS   Thank you for having the boys here.

LADY ASHBROOK	I couldn't be more delighted. I have long	15

LADY ASHBROOK   I couldn't be more delighted. I have long been an admirer of the Coram Hospital. We have emulated the Coram methods in our orphanage here at Ashbrook. Now, I thought you could perform in the drawing room.

THOMAS   Wherever you want us.   20

LADY ASHBROOK   I've brought in an instrument for you – a harpsichord.

THOMAS   Thank you.

Mrs Lynch has come outside.

LADY ASHBROOK   Let's get all these little chaps settled in, shall we? Boys! Boys! Follow Mrs Lynch,   25 please.

The Boys run inside. Lady Ashbrook, Alice and Melissa go too. Isobel can' t wait to speak to Thomas.

ISOBEL   How is he?

THOMAS   He's well. He's in Gloucester. He thought he should wait there until we know how things stand.   30

ISOBEL   Gloucester! So close. I can hardly bear it.

THOMAS   He just wants to come home. Do you think it's possible?

ISOBEL   I don't know. It all depends on Papa.

THOMAS   Is he here?   35

ISOBEL   He'll be back this evening. Thomas, he doesn't know about the concert.

THOMAS   I see.

ISOBEL	Mama decided not to tell him. I think … There's been such an awful silence these last eight years, such a terrible strain … 40
THOMAS	Yes.
ISOBEL	I know it puts you in a difficult position. Mama does too. If you want to turn around and go back … 45
THOMAS	No. I wouldn't dream of it.
ISOBEL	Oh, Thomas. Should we tell her about Alex? If there's going to be trouble, perhaps it's better that we tell her now.
THOMAS	Let's hold our nerve. See what happens tonight. 50

Melissa comes back outside.

MELISSA	Lady Ashbrook is asking where you want everything.
THOMAS	Right. Thank you.
MELISSA	Is Alexander all right? 55
ISOBEL	Yes. Why don't you write to him? Thomas could deliver the letter.
MELISSA	No. I have no call on his heart.
ISOBEL	But …
MELISSA	People change. We were practically children. 60
ISOBEL	But … you'll tell him about the baby?
MELISSA	I don't know. I don't know if I want to. I don't think it would be fair. I manage. I've managed for all these years.
ISOBEL	You must tell him. I'm sure he would want to know. 65

MELISSA It would have been his birthday today – our little Alex.

ISOBEL Oh, Melissa! Oh, that's terrible. How could I have forgotten?   70

MELISSA It's all right.

ISOBEL It must have been because of Thomas coming and ... I'm awful.

MELISSA It's all right. Darling, Isobel. No one could have been a more constant friend than you.   75

Scene 13

*In the **drawing room**, everything is being put in place for the concert. Melissa and Mrs Milcote have brought in drinks and cake for the Boys, who are eating happily. Thomas is supervising. Mrs Milcote, who looks rather ill and worn, passes close to Thomas.*

MELISSA Mother, you remember Thomas?

MRS MILCOTE Oh. Yes. Yes. How do you do?

THOMAS Well. Thank you.

Mrs Milcote moves away.

MELISSA I'm afraid she hasn't been in good health for some time.   5

THOMAS I'm very sorry to hear that.

Pause.

MELISSA The children are adorable.

THOMAS Yes. Most of the time.

MELISSA I look at the children in the orphanage sometimes and I marvel at them; at their   10

enthusiasm, their resilience, their hope.
There is so much we can learn from them.

Outside, Mish has come to peer in through the
window in search of Aaron. He sees Melissa and the
shock has a physical effect on him. He turns away.

THOMAS One of these boys is apprenticed to Alexander.

MELISSA To Alex? Which one?

THOMAS *(pointing to Aaron)* That one. 15

MELISSA I knew you would say that one.

THOMAS Aaron? Come here, please.

Aaron comes to them – wondering what he's done
wrong. But Melissa smiles warmly at him. Outside,
Mish looks through the window again. He sees
Melissa and Aaron together.

MELISSA Hello, Aaron.

AARON Hello, Miss.

MELISSA Have you had a cake? 20

AARON Yes, thank you, Miss.

MELISSA Well, you must have another. And how old
are you, Aaron?

AARON I'll be eight next week, Miss.

MELISSA Will you really? Eight. That's a lovely age. 25

Mish watches as she smooths Aaron's hair and
straightens his collar. Mish rushes away to a quiet
corner, panicking and distressed. For the first time
in eight years he feels the need to be dead. He lies
down on the ground and his eyes roll back into his
head. But terrible memories flood back to him, of

Otis's harsh voice and mothers wailing and babies crying.

MISH   Angel? Angel!

His Angel is suddenly there – but as he rushes towards her he suddenly stops. She is not smiling – she looks angry.

ANGEL   Tell him, Meshak.

MISH   No!

ANGEL   Tell him. Give him his mother. Give me my son.   30

MISH   No! No!

He wakes himself up. He sits up and cries.

You leave him! My Angel child. Mish Da. Mish Ma.

Scene 14

*That evening, in the **drawing room,** the Coram Boys give their concert. Thomas accompanies them on the harpsichord. All the Ashbrook Family, with the exception of Sir William are there, along with several Neighbours and local Dignitaries. Isobel throws anxious looks towards the door, watching for her father. Lady Ashbrook maintains complete composure.*

The moment comes for Aaron's solo – 'Oh Death, Where Is Thy Sting'. He stands and begins to sing. His voice is strikingly like Alexander's at the same age. What is more, he even looks like Alexander – particularly when he sings. All the Family notice it. It is almost too much for Lady Ashbrook. And Melissa

119

and Isobel find their minds full of thoughts of what might have been. But it is particularly shocking to Mrs Milcote. She rises from her chair for a moment, hardly able to breathe. Melissa looks at her in concern and draws her back down. But she continues to stare and to tremble.

At this moment, Sir William enters. He can hardly believe what he is seeing or hearing. But he is overwhelmed – at the sound of that voice. Lady Ashbrook and Isobel glance at him. It is impossible to know what he is thinking.

Just before the music finishes, Sir William strides from the room. Lady Ashbrook sees him go. Isobel and Thomas exchange a significant look.

When the concert ends, the Audience applaud warmly. Lady Ashbrook holds herself together to thank the Boys. Mrs Milcote sees Mrs Lynch and catches her arm.

MRS MILCOTE Did you hear him? The boy?

Mrs Lynch draws Mrs Milcote to one side. Melissa glances round and watches with concern.

Are you certain he is dead? Are you quite certain? He is so like Alexander.

The name seems to reverberate around the room. People turn and look at them.

MRS LYNCH *(whispering)* Do you or do you not pay me for my silence? 5

MRS MILCOTE Yes. But …

MRS LYNCH Then let us *be* silent.

Mrs Lynch walks away. Lady Ashbrook walks from the room.

Scene 15

*Lady Ashbrook rushes to find Sir William. He is standing in the **hallway**.*

LADY ASHBROOK   William?

SIR WILLIAM   How did this happen? Why did you allow this?

LADY ASHBROOK   Because I've seen you. I've seen you in church when the choir is singing. Look at   5
you. Your eyes have filled with tears now because of that boy's voice.

SIR WILLIAM   I feel it! Yes. I feel it. But that does not mean that I regret what I did. It does not mean that I relent or that my position has changed in   10 the slightest way.

LADY ASHBROOK   But why? Why? Why must we go on suffering like this? Nothing is worth this. I cannot bear it any longer! I'm sorry, but I cannot bear it. I cannot bear it.   15

She begins to cry, desperately. Sir William goes to her and holds her. Behind them, Thomas and Isobel enter.

Scene 16

*In her **bedroom**, Mrs Milcote is clutching the pink shawl which she found in the wood.*

MRS MILCOTE   Dear God. Dear God, can it be true?

Scene 17

*At **Mr Gaddarn's house**, Toby is polishing the floor.*
He sees a line of Girls approaching. They are being
led by two of Mr Gaddarn's Servants. They are
Coram Girls, and there are six of them. Toby is
immediately alarmed. He pulls back so as not to
be seen. The Girls pass by. He recognises one as
Molly Jenkins. She is smiling and excited.

TOBY   Molly!

MOLLY   Oh, no. Toby Gaddarn. You look awful! I'm
going to a big house in the country.

TOBY   No, Molly …

MOLLY   Out of my way, slave!   5

The Servant leads the Girls into the map room. Toby
follows at a distance. Inside the room, Mr Gaddarn
is waiting. Toby peers round the door, shaking with
fear. He is holding his mother's beads in his hand,
worrying them between his fingers.

GADDARN   Now, girls, let me show you to some
temporary accommodation. It's just for a day
or two.

He moves the big globe. A panel slides open in the
wall behind it, revealing the dark entrance to a
passageway. Toby's eyes grow wide.

One of the Servants steps into it.

Follow the man.

The Girls look suddenly fearful.

MOLLY   In there? But it's dark. And it's wet.   10

GADDARN   There's lights further down the passage.
Don't you worry now. Go on.

*Molly reluctantly goes in, followed by the other
Girls. Toby hears them call out:*

MOLLY   I don't like it in here!

GIRL   Can we go back?

Mr Gaddarn turns away and says to the other Servant.

GADDARN   Close it up when he's out. Feed 'em twice a day. 15

*Mr Gaddarn suddenly heads towards the door.
Toby starts and rushes away, but in his panic he
drops his mother's beads. He freezes. Mr Gaddarn
sees the beads and picks them up.*

GADDARN   Oh dear.

TOBY   Please can I have my mother's beads?

GADDARN   Come and get them, then.

Toby does not dare.

You know your mother's dead, don't you?
Slaves never last long. One day, soon now, I'll 20
sell you as a slave. Until then, I'll whip you
like one.

Toby runs.

Run, run, Toby Gaddarn.

Scene 18

*The following day, in the **drawing room** at Ashbrook.
Alexander is standing alone by the harpsichord. He
begins to play – a new piece of music he is writing.*

123

Suddenly Alice appears. She stops short when she sees him. Alexander stops playing.

ALICE   Are you him?

Alexander stares at her.

ALEXANDER Alice?

ALICE   Are you him? Are you …

SIR WILLIAM Alexander.

Alexander looks up. Sir William has entered behind Alice.

Yes, Alice. This is Alexander.   5

Father and son look at each other for several moments, then walk towards each other and embrace.

Lady Ashbrook and Isobel then come hurrying in and throw their arms around him. They are followed by Mrs Milcote and Melissa. Thomas stands in the doorway, beaming. Melissa hangs back as Everyone surrounds Alexander.

At the window, Mish appears. He sees Alexander and watches as Alexander's eyes meet Melissa's for the first time. His fear of losing Aaron intensifies.

Melissa holds Alexander's gaze for several moments, but then she leaves the room and the house. Mrs Milcote has been watching her and follows her outside.

MRS MILCOTE Melissa? Where are you going?

MELISSA   I can't … I'm sorry.

She walks off in the direction of Waterside. Mrs Milcote pursues her.

MRS MILCOTE   At least come back into the house! Melissa!

But Melissa disappears into the woods. Mrs Milcote turns to go back. Mish, who has followed Melissa's movements, is caught unawares and finds himself face to face with Mrs Milcote. They both freeze, and both are instantly taken back to the night of the baby's birth.

You!

Mish starts to run.

Wait! Wait! The baby! What happened to the   10
baby? Please …

Scene 19

*At **Waterside**, Melissa is sitting amongst the disused dolls and cradles. The door opens and Alexander walks in. They look at each other for some time before either can speak.*

ALEXANDER   Isobel told me you would be here. I should have known it anyway.

MELISSA   I'm very glad you've come home.

Pause.

ALEXANDER   You look well. Exactly as I remember you.

MELISSA   I don't think that can be true.   5

Pause.

ALEXANDER   Melissa … I thought of you. Every day. I want you to know that there was never anyone else … anyone who …

MELISSA Alex …

ALEXANDER I am not naive as I was then. I know I have no 10
right to expect anything. But if there remains
the slightest affection for me … in your heart
… I left my heart with you. Nothing has really
touched me since … I am asking for a chance
… a chance to … 15

MELISSA Stop, Alexander, please.

ALEXANDER You don't care for me. Of course.

MELISSA It's not …

ALEXANDER Is there someone else? Forgive me, I have no
right to … 20

MELISSA Yes.

*Alexander is astonished. It is like a physical blow
to him.*

No! That's not what I mean. Alex … after you
left … We had a child. There was a baby.
Stillborn. A boy.

Pause.

ALEXANDER We had a child. 25

MELISSA He was … stillborn. I'm sorry.

*At this moment, Isobel is heard calling as she runs
towards the cottage.*

ISOBEL Melissa! Melissa!

She bursts through the door.

Your mother. She's collapsed. Come quickly.

Scene 20

Evening. Mrs Milcote is lying in bed. She has not awoken since she collapsed. Melissa is sitting beside her, watching and worrying. Suddenly, Mrs Milcote stirs.

MRS MILCOTE   Melissa?

MELISSA   Mother. Mother. Thank God. Here.

She puts a glass of water to her mother's lips and she drinks a little.

MRS MILCOTE   Did they stop him?

MELISSA   Who?

MRS MILCOTE   Did they catch him?   5

MELISSA   Who? Mother, I don't know what you mean.

MRS MILCOTE   You have to find him. You have to bring him to me.

MELISSA   Who? Don't worry about anything now.

MRS MILCOTE   Meshak. His name was Meshak Gardiner.   10

MELISSA   Gardiner?

MRS MILCOTE   The son. The son.

MELISSA   You mean the son of that man who hanged? The murderer?

MRS MILCOTE   Oh, my Lord. My Lord.   15

MELISSA   Please don't get upset, Mother. The doctor said …

MRS MILCOTE   Is she listening?

MELISSA   Who? Do you mean Mrs Lynch?

MRS MILCOTE   She mustn't hear. She mustn't know I have told you.   20

MELISSA	She's not here, I swear it. Mother, has Mrs Lynch been ... has she been demanding money from you because of ... ?
MRS MILCOTE	Oh, my darling. Oh, my girl. My girl. 25
MELISSA	Why didn't you tell me? I have wanted to ask you so many times, but you made it so plain that you never wanted me to mention him.
MRS MILCOTE	Oh, my darling ... 20
MELISSA	I thought you must be disgusted with me.
MRS MILCOTE	Never. Never that. But you must listen to me now. Listen. There is another secret which she keeps. A secret which has eaten away at my soul so that I can hardly live. 35
MELISSA	What? You're frightening me.
MRS MILCOTE	You cannot forgive me, but please try to understand. I only ever did what I thought was right for you. Melissa, your baby ... he was not stillborn. He was not dead. I held 40 him and I felt his heart beating.

Melissa is silent.

He was alive. He was alive when we gave him to Otis Gardiner.

Melissa's blood runs cold.

MELISSA	Otis Gardiner?
MRS MILCOTE	He was meant to take him to the Coram 45 Hospital. But then we found the bodies in the woods ...
MELISSA	Oh, no ...

| MRS MILCOTE | I found my shawl – the shawl we wrapped your baby in. I found it. | 50 |

| MELISSA | No. |

| MRS MILCOTE | But Melissa, listen to me … |

| MELISSA | No. Oh, no. |

| MRS MILCOTE | The boy – the Coram boy – he is so like you. He is so like Alexander. And Meshak Gardiner was there. Do you see? That night. I saw him. And now he has come here with the boy. | 55 |

| MELISSA | What are you saying? |

| MRS MILCOTE | What if he took him? What if he saved your baby and took him to the Coram Hospital? | 60 |

Scene 21

*In the **kitchen**, the Coram Boys, with the exception of Aaron, are just sitting down to eat. Thomas is supervising. Melissa comes rushing in. She scans the Boy's faces.*

| THOMAS | Hello. How is she? |

| MELISSA | Where's Aaron? |

| THOMAS | Aaron. Yes. I was just thinking that myself. He's normally first at the table. |

| MELISSA | Where is he? | 5 |

| THOMAS | Boys, do you know where Aaron is? *(They take no notice)* Boys! Do any of you know where Aaron is? |

| BOY | He went off with Mish. |

| MELISSA | Mish? | 10 |

| THOMAS | Dear oh dear. When did they go? |

129

BOY   Ages ago.

MELISSA   Who's Mish? Who's Mish?!

THOMAS   Aaron's friend. Red-haired fellow. He came
along to ride shot and help with the horses.   15

Melissa has turned white.

MELISSA   Meshak.

THOMAS   Are you all right, Melissa?

Alexander enters.

ALEXANDER   Melissa? What's happening?

She looks at him.

MELISSA   Aaron. It's Aaron.

Scene 22

*In the **drawing room** at Ashbrook. Sir William, Lady
Ashbrook, Isobel, Melissa, Alexander and Thomas
are all sitting around a table. Isobel is holding
Melissa's hand. Alexander sits silently, trying to
make sense of everything that has happened.*

SIR WILLIAM   I have men combing every inch of the
countryside. And I have sent word to the
Coram Hospital.

THOMAS   I doubt he would take him back there. Not if
he doesn't want to be found.   5

LADY ASHBROOK   Where else might he go?

THOMAS   He must know Gloucestershire like the back
of his hand.

ISOBEL   At least we know that this Meshak cares for
Aaron.   10

There is a knock at the door and Mrs Lynch enters. She looks momentarily shocked when she sees the whole family confronting her, but she immediately recovers her composure.

MRS LYNCH   You wanted to see me, My Lady?

They are all staring at her with dislike and anger.

LADY ASHBROOK   Mrs Lynch …

SIR WILLIAM   Do you know anything at all about what happened to my grandson?

LADY ASHBROOK   *(to Sir William)* Wait. Please. Mrs Lynch, Melissa 15 and Isobel have told Sir William and I about the baby. They have also told us about your part in what happened that night.

Pause.

MRS LYNCH   Her mother and I agreed it was for the best.

LADY ASHBROOK   To tell a girl that her baby is dead when it is 20 not?

MRS LYNCH   What else could we do? What could she have done with it? Would you have been happy if she had brought it to you? No. You would have told them both to leave and hoped you 25 would never see them again.

LADY ASHBROOK   That is simply not true.

SIR WILLIAM   Do not be insolent, woman.

MRS LYNCH   And if you hadn't sent them away, he would have done. *(She indicates Sir William)* A man 30 who would disown his own son.

The Ashbrooks are utterly shocked. Lady Ashbrook is moved to defend Sir William.

LADY ASHBROOK	How dare you speak to Sir William in such a way?
MRS LYNCH	People like you do not forgive these things. I should know. You are very selective in your 35 compassion. You show a sort of sweeping mercy to those so far beneath you they don't matter, but when it comes to anything which might threaten your perfect world, then, then the iron gates come down. And love 40 counts for nothing. I gave her baby to the Coram Man because I believed he would take it where it would be cared for …
SIR WILLIAM	You really expect us to believe that?
MRS LYNCH	I had no idea what he did with those babies. 45
SIR WILLIAM	You were lying then and you're lying now. What else do you know about that night? What do you know about this boy Meshak?
MRS LYNCH	*(categorically)* I know nothing.
LADY ASHBROOK	I will try very hard to believe you, Mrs Lynch. 50 Until today you have never given me cause to doubt your word. But for you to demand money from Mrs Milcote in return for your silence, poor Mrs Milcote who must have been suffering unbearably, that is beyond 55 forgiveness. To make money from the suffering of others takes a particularly nasty human being. And I can no longer have you in my employ.
MRS LYNCH	I have no wish to remain in this house. As for 60 making money from the suffering of others, I think you will find it is something we all do …

SIR WILLIAM   Get out!

MRS LYNCH   The silk on your back, the sugar in your tea,   65
all of this – all wealth is built upon the
suffering of others.

SIR WILLIAM   My wife is the most charitable woman in this
county. Her orphanage is an example to
every parish for …   70

MRS LYNCH   She could fund five orphanages if she chose
to sell one ring on her finger.

SIR WILLIAM   Get out of my house!

MRS LYNCH   You people disgust me. I hope you will be
called to account one day.   75

She starts to go.

ALEXANDER   Philip Gaddarn. Does the name mean
anything to you?

She freezes in her tracks.

MRS LYNCH   No, it does not.

*He scrutinises her face. She holds his gaze. Then
she leaves the room. There is silence for a moment.
Her accusations and manner have stunned them.*

THOMAS   Why did you ask about Gaddarn?

ALEXANDER   Because that day at the concert … at Gaddarn's 80
house. I felt quite certain I'd seen him before.
And now I know who he is: Otis Gardiner.

SIR WILLIAM   Otis Gardiner hanged. On the gibbet at
Stroud. I saw it myself.

ALEXANDER   And yet there is a man living in London, a   85
benefactor of the Coram Hospital, who I would
swear is him. Who oversaw the hanging?

SIR WILLIAM	Claymore – the magistrate.
ALEXANDER	Could we speak to him?
LADY ASHBROOK	He has moved away.
ISOBEL	There was an awful business with his ward – she took her own life.

Pause. Melissa begins to cry, silently.

LADY ASHBROOK	But if this man is Otis Gardiner … you don't think Meshak would take the boy there?
SIR WILLIAM	He can't be Otis Gardiner, I tell you.

Pause.

THOMAS	What do we do?
ALEXANDER	I think we should go to London and talk to Mr Gaddarn. Whoever he is, or was, at this moment he's all we've got.

Alexander approaches Melissa and kneels down beside her.

I'll find him. I'll find our son.

She looks at him but cannot reach out to him.

Scene 23

*Mish is walking through **countryside** with Aaron. Over his shoulder, Mish has a shotgun. Mish suddenly stops and points.*

MISH	Look!

Aaron looks. It is London – spread out before them.

AARON	London! It's London.

He jumps down and hugs Mish.

	Oh, Mish, you are taking me home. Thank you. Thank you.
MISH	We're not going home.	5
AARON	I mean, to Mr Brook's.
MISH	No.
AARON	Or we can go to the hospital if you like. And Mr Ledbury could take me back. And we could ask about you coming too.	10
MISH	Angel child and Mish are finding Toby.
AARON	Toby?
MISH	We'll go on the big ship with Toby.
AARON	No. Mish, no. I don't want to go on a ship. I don't think it would work, looking for Toby's mother. He doesn't even know where she is.	15
MISH	Big ship. Across the dark ocean.
AARON	No, Mish. I don't want to. I want to go back to Mr Brook's.
MISH	No!	20
AARON	I want to do the singing. I'm going to miss the concert!

Mish suddenly grabs him hard and shakes him.

MISH	Angel child stays with Mish.
AARON	I will stay with you, but we have to go back.
MISH	Mish Ma, Mish Da.	25
AARON	You're hurting me!

MISH   They'll take you away. They'll beat Mish. They'll hurt Mish. Bad Mish. Bad, bad.

AARON   No, Mish. It'll be all right if you take me back. You're hurting me!   30

Mish suddenly needs to be dead. He collapses down onto the ground and his hands twitch and his eyes roll back.

Mish! Mish! Don't! What are you doing? Mish! I'll stay with you. I will. We'll go and get Toby. Don't, Mish. Don't.

Scene 24

Evening. Mrs Lynch is waiting in the map room. A Servant enters, closely followed by Mr Gaddarn: Otis Gardiner. On seeing Mrs Lynch, Otis stops in his tracks.

OTIS   Well, well. Mrs Lynch.

MRS LYNCH   *(indicating the Servant)* Tell him to go.

OTIS   There's no need.

He is staring at her, scrutinising her. The difference in their stations is very apparent.

I knew I'd see you again – one way or another.

MRS LYNCH   They're onto you.   5

OTIS   Who are?

MRS LYNCH   The Ashbrooks.

OTIS   The Ashbrooks?

MRS LYNCH   They asked me about Philip Gaddarn. I mean it. They know.   10

OTIS   *(to Servant)* Put a watch on the doors – front and back. If anyone comes near this house, you tell me.

The Servant nods and leaves.

How could the Ashbrooks know? I haven't been near Gloucester.   15

MRS LYNCH   The son has been in London. He's seen you. And Meshak is back.

OTIS   Meshak?

MRS LYNCH   Yes. Meshak! He's taken a boy. A boy they think is their grandson. It could be their grandson.   20 The Ashbrook baby. Do you remember? The night that Meshak disappeared?

OTIS   Jesus Christ! Jesus Christ!

MRS LYNCH   You have to get out.

OTIS   No!   25

MRS LYNCH   Yes, Otis! This is it. They are onto you. They won't let this go.

OTIS   What can they prove? People saw me hang. What are they going to do? Dig up the body of that other poor beggar? A body eight years   30 old!

MRS LYNCH   Half of this game is knowing when to quit and move on.

OTIS   I'm not leaving all this! Look at it! Don't you pretend you're not impressed!   35

MRS LYNCH   I can't help you – not this time!

The Servant suddenly appears.

OTIS   What?

SERVANT	They were at the back door, Sir.

Mish and Aaron step anxiously into the room. Mish/Meshak sees Otis and his heart almost stops beating.

AARON	Sorry, Sir. We didn't mean to be any trouble. We just wanted to see Toby. 40
OTIS	Hello, Meshak.

Meshak suddenly bolts for the door, but the Servant grabs him and slams him against a wall.

AARON	Mish! Get off him! Help! Toby! Help! Toby … !

Otis grabs Aaron under his arm and stifles his mouth. Meshak is still struggling.

MESHAK	No!

The Servant has grabbed the shotgun off him and he now hits him in the face with it.

OTIS	You just couldn't do it, could you? You couldn't crawl into a ditch and die? 45

Outside the room, Toby has heard Aaron's cry and has started to head towards it. He is covered in cuts and bruises. There is blood all down his shirt and whip marks on his back. He peers around the door and sees Aaron and Meshak, captives.

(To Servant) Open the passage. We'll take them straight out there.

MRS LYNCH	Think what you're doing. Think now, Otis.
OTIS	They couldn't have timed it better. The ship's sailing tonight. 50

MRS LYNCH   What ship?

The Servant pushes the globe and the entrance to the passageway opens. From in the passageway the Girls' voices start up:

GIRLS   Let us out! Help us, please!

Otis watches the amazed look on Mrs Lynch's face and grins.

OTIS   Welcome to my world.

The Servant and Otis pull Meshak and Aaron into the passage. Mrs Lynch follows. She covers her nose and mouth to keep out the smell. They pass the Coram Girls, dirty and pale with terror. They reach out to them. Some of them wail louder when they recognise Meshak and Aaron. Mrs Lynch pauses and stares at them.

Scene 25

*Out on the street, Alexander and Thomas are just approaching **Mr Gaddarn's house**.*

THOMAS   This is the one.

Toby comes hurtling out of the front door of the house. There is a Servant there who grabs him.

SERVANT   No you don't.

But Toby bites him hard and the Servant lets go of him, shrieking with pain. Toby reaches the street and looks this way and that, panicking, not sure where to go, but knowing he must tell someone. He is about to run off, when Thomas calls to him:

THOMAS   Toby!

Toby looks round, terrified. But when he sees Thomas he runs towards him.

Toby? My God, what's happened to you?

TOBY   He's got them. Aaron and Mish.   5

ALEXANDER   Gaddarn?

Toby nods and tries to catch his breath.

THOMAS   Come on.

They are about to head into the house but Toby stops them.

TOBY   No! I know where he's taking them. To the docks. Through the passage. I know where it comes out.   10

THOMAS   Show us.

Scene 26

*At **the docks**. Otis, Mrs Lynch, the Servant, Meshak and Aaron are just emerging at the end of the tunnel from the house. Ahead of them now, they can see the River Thames and a ship moored very close by.*

But suddenly Alexander, Thomas and Toby come running up. They stop when they see the extreme danger of the situation. The Servant still has the shotgun. And Alexander is shocked to see Mrs Lynch. But the sight of his son being roughly held, and his terrified face, make Alexander recklessly brave.

ALEXANDER	That boy is my son. Let him go.
OTIS	You just back off, Mister.
THOMAS	We know who you are, Gaddarn.
ALEXANDER	Let him go! You won't escape. Let them both go. I'll speak for you. I'll save you from the gallows.
OTIS	I'm going nowhere near the gallows.
ALEXANDER	*(approaching steadily)* Aaron, I'm your father. Don't be afraid. It will be all right …

5

Alexander suddenly makes a grab for Aaron. The Servant raises the gun but Meshak begins to struggle like an angry bull and it is all he can do to control him. Alexander and Otis are locked in a struggle. Alexander manages to push him aside and is about to take hold of Aaron when Otis pulls a knife.

THOMAS	Alexander!

10

Alexander looks round in time to see the blade coming at him. Thomas throws himself in front of Alexander and takes the blow. He falls to the ground.

ALEXANDER	Thomas … Thomas!

A blow comes down on Alexander's head. He falls and hits his head on the stone ground. He is unconscious.

AARON	No!

The Servant from the front of the house runs up.

OTIS	Get them on the ship. I'll go back for the girls.

*The Servants lead Meshak and the Boys away. Otis
turns to pick up the gun, but Mrs Lynch grabs it
first. She turns it on him.*

What's this?

MRS LYNCH Leave the girls.   15

*He goes to walk past her. She pulls the trigger
back.*

OTIS What's this? Bit late to find your conscience,
ain't it?

MRS LYNCH It's a mess, Otis, and I don't like mess. Now
you're getting on that ship, without them
and without me.   20

OTIS No! Do you know how much those girls are
worth?

MRS LYNCH *(threatening him)* I'll do it.

OTIS Money then. I've got money in there. Let me
get it. How much do you want?   25

MRS LYNCH You have five seconds to get onto that ship
before I scream for help. One …

OTIS You're mad! Do you want to get caught?

MRS LYNCH I never get caught. Two. Three. Four … I'm
sorry, Otis. Five. *(Shouting)* Help! Help here!   30
I need help! Help!

OTIS You're mad! I hope you rot in hell.

*He runs off to the ship. She stops shouting and
watches him go. Alexander begins to stir. Mrs Lynch
walks off, in the opposite direction from the ship.*

Scene 27

*Meshak, Aaron and Toby are on **the deck of the ship**. Meshak is dizzy and weak from the blows he has received. Aaron and Toby run from one rail to another, staring in horror at the water around them.*

AARON   Mish! We're heading out to sea!

TOBY   They'll make me a slave.

AARON   *(to Meshak)* It's your fault. All of it. All of it.

MESHAK   *(crying)* Sorry. Sorry.

TOBY   We've got to jump.   5

AARON   *(dismayed)* We're too far out. I can't do it.

TOBY   We've got to. I won't be a slave. I can't be a slave, Aaron.

Otis appears. He laughs when he sees them.

OTIS   Fancy a swim, do you?

AARON   *(unsure what to do)* Mish?   10

Toby climbs up on the rail as Otis approaches him.

OTIS   *(walking towards him)* Don't want to be a slave, eh? Go on then. What's stopping you?

He grabs hold of Toby and throws him over the side.

AARON   Toby, no!

Aaron climbs the rail and jumps over too.

MESHAK   No!

He rushes at Otis and hurls him to the ground. The two of them struggle. Meshak gets his hands

round Otis's neck. Otis draws his knife and stabs
Meshak in the stomach. Meshak feels suddenly
weak. Otis scrambles away from him and looks
aghast when he sees the blood pouring from him.
Meshak looks up at him.

Da?   15

Otis cannot speak.

Da?

He staggers to his feet and lurches to the rails,
where Aaron and Toby went in.

OTIS   Don't, Meshak! Don't be a fool!

But Meshak throws himself overboard. On the
deck, Otis sinks to his knees. He feels utterly
wretched and sick.

In the water, Meshak, Aaron and Toby are fighting
for their lives. None of them can swim. Meshak,
though badly injured, desperately tries to push
the Boys upwards to the surface.

The water begins to whisper Meshak's name.
A strange light begins to shine around him. With
one last, enormous effort he pushes the Boys up.
He lets go of Toby and then Aaron.

MESHAK   Angel …

And the Boys are gone, and his Angel is there in
front of him. She smiles and opens her arms.

ANGEL   Come now, Meshak. Come to me.

The light grows. She swoops down over him and
he feels the absolute joy of her embrace.

Scene 28

*Christmas Eve. In the **chapel** at the Coram Hospital, the Choir are taking their places to sing Messiah. Handel is sitting at the organ.*

Sir William and Lady Ashbrook are sitting on the front row of the packed and excited Audience. Mrs Milcote is sitting beside them, followed by Alice. Isobel is sitting with Thomas, whose arm and chest are bandaged as a result of his wound. They are all dressed in black and all look sad and strained. Melissa keeps looking round anxiously.

HANDEL Where is our conductor, eh? Mr Brook?

The Boys look around for him.

The Messiah cannot wait. It is almost Christmas!

Some of the Audience laugh, but the Ashbrooks look at each other with concern. Melissa stands.

MELISSA Excuse me.

She walks towards the door of the chapel. Then she spots Alexander. He is sitting alone in a secluded corner. She goes to him.

Alex?   5

He looks up at her.

ALEXANDER I can't do it.

She sits down next to him.

I keep picturing Meshak's body … the way it looked when they pulled him from the water.

And then I think of Aaron … and I wonder if … somewhere … 10

MELISSA Don't.

ALEXANDER And Toby. It could all have been so different.

Pause.

MELISSA We have to try. We have to try to find a way to live.

ALEXANDER Why did this happen? Was it our fault? 15

MELISSA No.

ALEXANDER Did we do something so very wrong?

MELISSA No. We did nothing wrong. I loved you, Alex. I love you still.

He looks at her and they embrace. Holding each other desperately.

Everyone's waiting. 20

Alexander nods. They start to walk towards the Choir. Mrs Hendry hurries up behind them.

MRS HENDRY Mr Brook? There are two boys at the door – late arrivals – they want to know if they can still join in.

ALEXANDER I'm afraid not. I think we must begin now …

MELISSA Alex … 25

He turns and follows her gaze. Slowly, from out of the light, Aaron and Toby come walking towards them, hand in hand. They look dishevelled and tired but otherwise no worse for wear. They reach them. Alexander takes Aaron's hands, as if he might not be real.

ALEXANDER Aaron, Aaron.

The Ashbrooks and Thomas slowly stand, unable to believe what they are seeing.

AARON Is it true, Sir? Are you my father?

ALEXANDER Yes. Yes, I am.

AARON But what about Mish?

ALEXANDER Mish ... was your father too. But he's with   30
the angels now. He'll be your guardian angel.
Always. Do you understand?

AARON I think so.

MELISSA Hello, Aaron.

ALEXANDER This ... Aaron, this beautiful lady is your   35
mother.

Aaron looks at Melissa.

AARON But I haven't got a mother, Sir.

MELISSA Yes you have. Yes you have. *(to Toby)* And I
could be your mother too – if you'd like.

Toby hugs her. Melissa and Alexander put their arms around Aaron and Toby and hold them tight.

HANDEL Mr Brook! You choose a very inconvenient   40
time to discover your joy.

AARON Could you let go of me now, please? I'm
sorry, but I really have to sing.

ALEXANDER Go, Aaron. Go and sing.

Aaron goes and takes his place in the Coram Choir. Alexander hugs Melissa one last time before leaving her with Toby and going to conduct Messiah – with great, great, joy.

Otis, Meshak, Miss Price and her baby, Mercy

Otis, Meshak and Mercy

Melissa with Alexander's letter

Mrs Lynch, Mrs Milcote, Isobel, Melissa and Melissa's baby

Meshak in the water

Alexander, Melissa, Aaron and Toby

Introduction to the Activities

The drama activities and approaches will help you come to a greater understanding of the textual features and dramatic structures in *Coram Boy*. They explore the writing process, style and writer's technique as well as the thematic, content-based issues and ideas. You will develop your analytical skills as well as the capacity to apply this critical thinking to other texts, ideas or issues.

The active nature of the activities and the critical thinking developed demand that you explore and respond to the play both in relation to its staging and performance, as well as in relation to the original Jamila Gavin novel from which it has been adapted. Exploring and analysing the adaptation process allows you to examine the decisions, techniques and imagination required to move it from prose to script and from page to stage.

It is intended that, rather than working independently, you will collaborate in pairs and groups throughout under the guidance of your teacher. It is important that you are aware of the learning process and understand the aims and objectives of each session. Recording your thinking will help to inform the work and written responses as they develop.

From the initial planning to the final staging and performance of the play, the activities described can become an important part of the performance process.

An understanding of the writer's techniques, adaptation, the decision-making process and the roles of the writer, playwright, director and audience has a direct impact on the way in which actors and non-actors can approach a performance of the script.

The activities offered here provide a structure, which enables you to build on your learning and understanding. Although the approaches are related to specific scenes and aspects of the play, the conventions and techniques can clearly be used in relation to other aspects of the play and/or other texts.

Paul Bunyan and Ruth Moore

Activity 1: What do children need?

Learning outcomes

You will:

- question what children need most
- develop your understanding of society in the play
- develop your understanding of symbolism and props in the play
- listen to, organise and present ideas.

You will do this by reorganising words into a quotation from the play and selecting objects that are associated with the different words.

1 Sit in a large circle. In the centre will be a number of objects – e.g. a shawl, candle, ribbons and pictures – surrounding a wicker (Moses) basket. Your teacher will give you each a card with a word such as 'poor', 'of' and 'citizens' written on it.

2 Moving round the circle, each student reads out their word. Once the words have been read, think carefully about what order they might go in to make sense as one quotation. Through discussion and negotiation, re-position the words around the circle so they can be read out in the 'correct' order.

3 Read out the words again in your new position. What do you think this quotation means? Why might it be important when studying the play?

4 Choose another word in the circle that you think connects to yours. This might be a word that helps to give emphasis to yours, such as 'is' or 'its', or it might be a word that you feel links with yours in some way, such as 'children' with 'society'. Pair up with the student who has that word, sitting next to them but remaining in the large circle. (If your first choice has been taken by another student, then select the next best word to pair with yours.)

5 As a pair, choose one of the objects from the centre of the circle that you think provides some meaning to the words you have selected.

6 Your teacher will sit in the centre of the circle as a character, with the Moses basket. One pair at a time, you will be asked to bring the object out to the character, with the basket, that your teacher is playing. As you do, complete and say out loud the phrase 'Children need ...', and present your object to the character in what you feel is the most appropriate way. Music may be played while everyone in the circle completes this task.

What have I learnt?

- What skills have you used/developed in this activity?
- What have you learnt about some of the issues that might be explored in the play?
- How did choosing an object help you to think about the use of symbolism and props in the play?

Activity 2: Setting a context and exploring the setting

Learning outcomes

You will:

- analyse pictures
- investigate, in role, the context and setting of the play
- describe and explain accurately
- listen to and select information.

You will do this by exploring the world of Gloucester Cathedral and being introduced to a character through the **Teacher in Role** convention.

Teacher in Role: a crucial technique whereby the group leader adopts a role (which could be central to the drama) that offers a model of appropriate language and behaviour. Sometimes the teacher will deliberately choose a low-status role to offer an alternative perspective.

1   Look at the pictures of Gloucester Cathedral. Discuss what sort of place it is.

2   Now look around the room at the various pictures or objects that might be found in Gloucester Cathedral. These will include a picture of a stained glass window of an angel and pictures of religious sculptures. Some of the pictures might have short pieces of text that accompany them.

3   What can you see in the pictures? What sort of place is it? What significance might each object/picture have?

4   Imagine you are visiting the cathedral and the objects in it for the first time. In groups of four, you are going to use the **Overheard Conversation** convention to 'explore' this space. As you move around the space, as if within the walls of the cathedral, and approach each object, you will comment on what you see and hear, have a conversation about the place you are in, or ask each other questions. However, the conversation and movement can only begin once it is being 'overheard' by the character the teacher adopts. Your teacher will move around the space, approaching a group at a time. Once s/he approaches your group, you can come to life, move and talk, as the conversation is being 'overheard' but once s/he moves away you must stop and become silent again.

Overheard Conversation: a character in the drama is identified and witnessed eavesdropping on other characters' conversations. The device may be a means of evidencing testimony or gossip or may be a means of linking group work together as in the case of the **Teacher in Role** as the eavesdropper reporting back in narration or at the end of a dramatic sequence.

5 Move into a new space with your group next to a picture. You will be given some time to rehearse your conversation in your groups before your teacher adopts the role. Your teacher will narrate some words adapted from Act One, Scene 1 (page 7):

> My name is Meshak Gardiner. I am fourteen years old, strange-faced, large-limbed, tattered and hungry. As I enter the cathedral, I look about nervously and listen. At the other end the choirboys are practising. I begin my journey down the south aisle. I feel like I shouldn't be here, but I have just enough courage left to move forward, past the gargoyles ...

As the teacher in role walks towards a group, they begin their Overheard Conversation. In between visiting different groups, the teacher will add further narration, adapted once again from Act One, Scene 1 (pages 7–8):

Extract 1: A sudden loud burst of playing on the organ sends me scuttling for cover behind a stone pillar, but as soon as it stops I emerge again and continue.

Extract 2: I am almost there now. I can see her – my angel. I feel she is calling to me, whispering my name – 'Meshak'. She is tucked away in a side chapel, inconspicuous, but to me she is a beacon – the most beautiful thing I have ever seen or could possibly imagine. I reach her and stare up at her – the sculpture with glowing auburn hair, the bluest eyes and the kindest expression.

6   Once the teacher in role has heard each group's conversation, freeze while s/he reads:

> The music washes over me. I stand in front of the angel and begin to sing a phrase I have just heard from the choirboy's solo. Suddenly behind me a choirboy appears and sings the same phrase. I look round, terrified at having been caught. The boy stares at me. For a moment there is a strange sense of sameness and recognition between us.

What have I learnt?

- What skills have you used/developed in this activity?
- How were you able to develop your conversations with integrity?
- What did you use to help you do this?
- What have you learnt about the setting, characters and context of the play?

Activity 3: Exploring the characters of Meshak and Alexander

Learning outcomes

You will:

- investigate the characters of Meshak and Alexander
- select appropriate information
- organise and present ideas.

You will do this by analysing extracts from the play and making reasoned judgements about the information you are given.

1   As a class, look back at the extracts used by your teacher in Activity 2.

2   Sit in a large semi-circle and look at the large stained glass projection of an angel.

3 Use the **Role on the Object** convention to explore the character of Meshak. To do this you need to identify from these extracts what you know about Meshak and choose a word you feel best describes him. Your teacher will write this word on a piece of card and give it to you. Put your word onto the image of the angel. Think carefully about where you might place it according to the colour beneath it.

Role on the Object: to help define character traits at particular moments in drama, an object or image is placed in front of the participants. Statements or words written on cards are placed by the students who have identified them on or around the object.

---

3 Repeat the exercise to explore the character of Alexander.

You will return to the **Role on the Object** at different stages in the play to add new words and discuss previous choices. You may want to record your responses, ideas and comments about the play as a whole, on the image, in the same way described above. This will provide a useful prompt and recap tool and give you a valuable resource when you are planning your written responses to the text.

What have I learnt?

- What analytical skills have you developed in this activity?
- How did you decide what words to choose for Meshak and Alexander?
- Do you think this description will remain throughout the whole play? Why?
- How does placing the words on the different colours add to their meaning?
- How might this activity help with your understanding of the playwright's use of colour, sounds and symbols?

Activity 4: Investigating the play – meeting the Coram Man

Learning outcomes

You will:

- develop the use of space, facial expression, gesture and tone
- investigate and analyse the script
- question critically the ideas and issues introduced at this stage of the play.

You will do this by investigating the extract and considering how the script might be staged in order to produce **Digital Video Clips**.

> **Digital Video Clip:** a short, repeatable dramatic sequence is 'bookended' with a **Still Image** at the start and a **Still Image** at the end.

1   Working in groups of three to five, you will be allocated an extract from Act One, Scene 5 (see below and pages 18–25).

Extract 1: lines 1–18 from Act One, Scene 5 (page 20)

| *from* | MRS LYNCH | Where have you been? |
| *to* | OTIS | Oh I'm ready. |

Extract 2: stage instruction following line 18 to line 35, Act One, Scene 5 (pages 20–22)

| *from* | | *They enter the room …* |
| *to* | MISS PRICE | Tell me please … tell me about Thomas Coram. |

Extract 3: lines 36–64, Act One, Scene 5 (pages 22–23)

| *from* | OTIS | Thomas Coram? Oh, he's a kind and gentle man … |
| *to* | OTIS | By the kindest of women. Women who know about babies. |

Extract 4: lines 65–78, Act One, Scene 5 (page 23)

from	Mrs Lynch	Then when they're old enough, they are taken to live at the hospital.
to	Miss Price	Her name is mercy.

Extract 5: stage instruction following line 79 to line 80, Act One, Scene 5 (page 23)

from		*There is a long pause.*
to	Mrs Lynch	Can you be sure that Coram will take the child?

Extract 6: lines 104–116, Act One, Scene 5 (pages 24–25)

from	Otis	I understand, Miss.
to	Otis	On my son's life, I swear it.

2   In your group, produce a short **Digital Video Clip** of your allocated extract. To do this, begin with a **Still Image**, followed by an **Action Reading** of the script, then freeze at the end in a final **Still Image**. You will need to investigate the script and search for clues about the characters, story and setting so that you can produce an accurate **Action Reading**.

Still Image/Still Picture/Freeze-Frame: a Still Image is created by participants in the drama standing motionless, often at a given sign by the teacher or as a result of being sculpted by other students into the frozen image. This convention is used to mark a significant moment or enable time for reflection.

Action Reading: students, in role, walk through a scene, speaking lines and adding gestures and movements, while reading from scripts.

---

3 As a class, produce your **Digital Video Clips** as **Rolling Theatre**. Appropriate music such as Handel's 'Foundling Hospital Anthem' could be used to guide you.

All groups freeze in their initial **Still Image**. The first group unfreezes, adds the action, then freezes again. When they freeze, the next group knows that they can begin. This continues with all the groups producing their **Digital Video Clip**. When you are not presenting your **Digital Video Clip**, you can become a **Spect-actor**. This means that while your body is frozen in the **Still Image**, your head turns to follow the action so that you can see and hear the work of other groups. You should remain in your place, in order for all the groups to freeze in their final **Still Image** at the end.

> **Rolling Theatre:** a means by which groups can share their work on different aspects of a drama, learning from each other by running several rehearsed sections in a sequence.

> **Spect-actor:** participants in a performed element of a drama session also become spectators and follow the action with their eyes and heads when the focus is not directly upon them.

What have I learnt?

- How did performing these extracts help you to gain an understanding of the issues, characters and setting?
- How did you use space, gestures, tone, pace and facial expressions during the **Digital Video Clip**?
- What have you learnt about the characters and events in the play?

Activity 5: Exploring tension – fact meets fiction at the orphanage

Learning outcomes

You will:

- explore the historical context and issues in the play
- investigate and analyse the script, selecting relevant information and explore the ideas presented
- present an argument effectively, using evidence to support your ideas.

You will do this through the use of a **Meeting Convention** to question the need to develop the orphanage on the Ashbrook Estate.

Meeting Convention: a group is gathered together in role to receive new information, agree action or solve problems. The meeting may be chaired by teacher in role, student in role or in some cases be deliberately convened with no identified leader.

---

1 As a class, explore some historical information, pictures and artefacts relating to Coram Hospital and Sir Thomas Coram. You might like to visit www.foundlingmuseum.org.uk to find key information.

2 Working in groups of four or five, you will be given a short extract from the novel of *Coram Boy*, which describes the people of the parish gathering at Ashbrook House to discuss the poor of the parish and the problems with the orphanage. Use your extract and the information gained in Task 1 of this activity to provide arguments that you will put to the meeting. Your teacher will explain the position that your group will take and therefore which arguments you will need to develop. The seating arrangement will suggest the space where the meeting will take place.

3 The teacher in role as Mr Claymore begins the meeting and explains the purpose of the gathering, by reading aloud the following extract adapted from the novel, Chapter 6 (page 77):

We are gathering here today at Ashbrook Hall to discuss the poor of the parish and the orphanage in particular, something which I know is a great concern of Lady Ashbrook's. There is more pressure than ever on the almshouses and the orphanage. No matter what we do, the poor never get fewer. Their presence is everywhere, not just on the streets of the city but in the countryside. We need to decide what we are going to do about it.

4 Using the **Meeting Convention**, contribute your ideas and arguments, using the evidence you have found, both from the historical material and the novel. Listen carefully to the views of others and decide how you can best present your case.

5 At the end of the meeting, your teacher will read out Gaddarn's words from lines 19–23, Act Two, Scene 9 (page 107), which were introduced at the very beginning of the workshop. The extract may also be projected onto a wall.

The way a nation treats its poor and unfortunate citizens, most especially its children, is a mark of how civilised it truly is. And I say, looking about me this afternoon, England is civilised indeed!

What have I learnt?

- What evidence did you use to decide on the position you took?
- What did you feel were the most successful aspects of your argument? Why?
- How did this activity help you to understand the historical context of the play and the issues involved?

Activity 6: Visiting the orphanage – the missing scene

Learning outcomes

You will:

- develop analytical skills
- investigate the motivation and thoughts of particular characters
- develop your understanding of the writer's and playwright's techniques and intentions.

You will do this by analysing a particular scene in the novel that has not been included in the play.

1 Working in groups of four, you will be given a short extract from Chapter 6 (pages 80–84) of the novel, which describes Lady Ashbrook's visit to the orphanage. This scene is not included in the play.

   from   Barely a week or a month had gone by ...
   to   ... there is nothing more to be done here.

2 As a group, choose a line from the extract that you feel is most important and illustrates the tension created (either in the character's own head or the scene) by her visit. Produce a **Still Image** to illustrate the line you have chosen. Write out the line on a large sheet of paper in front of your image.

3 Think about how the line might be said while the **Still Image** is being held. Would you say it as a group? Use echo? Whisper? Say it individually? What tone would you use and why?

4 Groups hold their **Still Images** and take it in turn to say their lines, producing a **Tableau** of the most significant aspects of the visit.

Tableau: a multi-dimensional frozen picture usually involving a number of actors depicting a significant image.

5   Discuss as a group why you think the playwright chose not to include this scene.

What have I learnt?

- What helped you to decide on the line and what helped you create the **Still Image**?
- How has this activity helped you to think about the character's motivation?
- How might this activity help you to question the nature of adaptation and the choices that are made?

Activity 7: Lady Ashbrook's conscience

Learning outcomes

You will:

- explore the tension in the play
- make reasoned judgements, and organise and present your ideas
- investigate and analyse the text to identify the character's thoughts and motivation.

You will do this by using the **Conscience Alley** convention to explore the tension in the scene and the motivation of the character.

> **Conscience Alley:** a group divided into two lines facing each other. A pupil (or teacher) in role as a character in the drama walks between the two lines as individuals speak out what is in the character's conscience. Each line might represent opposing perspectives.

Your teacher will read an extract from Chapter 6 (page 84) of the novel, describing how Lady Ashbrook rides away from the orphanage. It may also be projected.

As they rode swiftly away, they noticed a couple of thin young boys gathering firewood in the copse. Their bones stuck out through their thin shirts and one coughed all the time … Perhaps, since giving birth to her own children, she had become more aware of the welfare of the young.

1 As a class, stand in two parallel lines facing each other down the length of the room. Your teacher will stand in between these lines at one end of the room looking down the lines.

2 The teacher will adopt the role of Lady Ashbrook. As she walks down in between the two lines, she will hear her conscience speaking to her. One line of students will speak the thoughts of Lady Ashbrook as a mother; the other will speak her thoughts as the wife of a wealthy landowner.

3 As your teacher comes level with you, speak her thoughts out loud thinking carefully about the text you have just explored and what you feel are the character's motivations. Speaking as the mother, you might say: 'What if I hadn't been so fortunate and it was Alexander in there. What would I feel then?' Speaking as the wife, you might say: 'We give more money than lots of people around here and after all it is down to the poor themselves whether they work hard or not.' You will be given an opportunity to discuss with other students and rehearse what you are going to say. You must speak in the first person to narrate her thoughts.

What have I learnt?

- How does this activity help you to explore the tension and different aspects of a character that exist in the novel and play?
- How does such an activity help the actor prepare for the staging of other scenes in the play?
- What helped you to decide on Lady Ashbrook's thoughts?

Activity 8: Using Communal Voice to explore the tensions

Learning outcomes

You will:

- explore the relationship between sons and fathers in the play
- analyse the significance of the music in the play
- demonstrate an understanding of the drama process.

You will do this by using **Communal Voice** to question the tensions that exist between the father and his son.

Communal Voice: individual members of the group take up positions, one at a time, behind a sculpted character and speak the words that the character says at a chosen moment in the drama.

---

1 Read from the stage instruction before line 1 to line 13 from Act One, Scene 14 (pages 49–50):

from		*Sir William is walking to his study. Alexander runs up behind him.*
to	ALEXANDER	But I have to go on studying music. How can I do that if I come back here?

2 A member of the class is given the role of Sir William. Sculpt him into the position you believe he will be in when the action takes place.

Sculpting: participants offer suggestions while placing an individual in a significant, frozen position so that considered analysis can be made.

---

3   Another member of the class is given the role of Alexander. He is sculpted into the scene and freezes while your teacher and another student read lines 14–19, Act One, Scene 14 (page 50):

SIR WILLIAM   A bargain is a bargain. I made a bargain with you – against my better judgement, mind – but I stuck to it and you will stick to it too. Music is all very well for your friend in there, but it won't do for you.

ALEXANDER   But ...

4   Remaining students are asked who they think would speak next and what they would say. When you (or another student) suggest the next line to be spoken, the characters remain frozen while you move to stand behind the one you will speak for. The end of the extract is reread, after which you speak the next line. The remaining members of the class are then asked what they think the characters would say next. Individual students go and stand by the characters they think they can speak for.

5   The scene is frozen again, after your teacher explains that one by one the people behind the sculpted characters will continue the scene by speaking what they say or their thoughts. Using **Communal Voice**, continue the conversation between Sir William and Alexander, remembering that at times there may be silences.

What have I learnt?

- How does this activity help you to explore the tensions that exist in the play?
- What is the significance of music in Alexander's life and the play?
- What helped you to decide on what the characters would say? What skills did you need?

Activity 9: Placing the text

Learning outcomes

You will:

- write for a specific audience, with a specific purpose
- select appropriate information from the text
- explore the themes and tensions in the play
- organise and present your ideas appropriately.

You will do this by producing and placing pieces of text into the scene and making a contribution to the drama.

Placing the text: participants create two paper copies of a text which could be found in a defined space in the drama. One copy is placed in the appropriate place; the other is retained by its authors. When a student/teacher in role picks up, points to or unfolds each placed text, the authors of that text read its contents out loud, providing an insight to a key character's world.

---

1   As a class, read Act One, Scenes 22 and 23 (pages 70–72).

2   Your teacher will read extracts 1 and 2, and may also project them.

Extract 1: stage instruction before line 2 to line 4, Act One, Scene 25 (page 74)

from		*Sir William bursts from the drawing room into the hallway with a letter* ...
to	Sir William	It's Alexander. He's gone.

Extract 2: stage instruction before line 1, Act One, Scene 26 (page 75)

At Waterside, *Melissa walks in and sees the broken virginals. She is horrified. Next to it she sees a note. She rushes to it and picks it up. It has her name on it. She opens it with trembling hands and reads it.*

3 Working in groups of three, your teacher will give you the name of a character in the play that you will write a letter to, from Alexander before he leaves. The characters will include Thomas, Melissa, Lady Ashbrook, Sir William, Edward, Alice and Dr Smith (choirmaster).

4 In your group, write the letter that he would have written. It is important that you write two identical versions of this piece of text. Remember that you need to write in role as Alexander throughout the letter.

When you have finished the letter, decide which member of your group will adopt the role of the character who receives it. Think about how you might sculpt this character into the scene on the Ashbrook Estate and where you might place the letter they receive.

5 Sitting in a large semi-circle, the teacher will ask the first group to sculpt the character within the centre and position one copy of their letter. This process continues around the circle until all the characters have been sculpted and letters positioned. Once all the pieces of text have been placed, the sculpted characters gradually come to life. One at a time, they turn to, look at, and/or open the letters that have been written for them. As they come across the piece of text, they look at the text and freeze. If your group placed this particular character and letter, read it out now from the identical copy you have retained. You need to think about how you will read the text aloud in terms of the tone, style and pace. Read the letter as a pair or individually. The drama continues but stops while different students read out each letter – until they have all been read. Music may be used to introduce and close the sequence.

What have I learnt?

- What skills did you need to produce a piece of text that could be placed in the scene?
- What helped you to decide how to read out your piece of text?
- How might this activity help you to explore the tensions and themes of the play?

169

Activity 10: Exploring the adaptation process – from novel to script

Learning outcomes

You will:

- analyse the decisions and techniques used during the adaptation process
- select, organise and present relevant information and ideas in script and performance
- develop analytical skills and explore the writer's intentions
- consider the difficulties in staging such a scene.

You will do this by analysing a specific aspect of the novel, how it might be adapted for the stage and the issues that might arise.

1 As a class, sit in a semi-circle with the text available. Your teacher reads or plays a recording of the following projected extract from Chapter 2 (pages 20–22) of the novel:

> The light of his lantern swung a yellow shaft across the canvas ... He vomited against a tree, leaning his head into the bark so that it left its imprint on his brow.

2 Discuss what issues might need to be considered when adapting this for the stage.

Activity 11: Placing the writer and the reader

Learning outcomes

You will:

- analyse authorial intention and techniques, and explore the role of the reader and empathy in the text
- select and present evidence from the text to justify your comments
- listen to viewpoints and question critically.

You will do this by placing the writer and reader into a particular scene in order to explore the intentions and techniques employed.

> **Placing the Author/Writer:** in order to help students to appreciate an author's perspective, a student or teacher represents the presence, at a defined moment in the drama, of the author.

> **Placing the Audience/Reader:** a similar process to **Placing the Author** but here a student or teacher represents the presence and/or perspective of the audience or reader at a defined moment in the drama.

1 Look at Chapter 2 (page 22) in the novel when Meshak drops the live baby in the hole:

> Meshak let go the feebly moving bundle.

2 A member of the class is given the role of Meshak, while the rest form a circle around him. In turns, sculpt Meshak into the position you believe he will be in, using the space inside the circle. You could use a blanket to represent the baby. Think carefully about the facial expression Meshak might have. Other students may question your positioning and can re-sculpt Meshak into a position of their choosing.

3 Another member of the class is given the role of Otis. The character is sculpted into the scene and frozen while the following extract from Chapter 2 (page 22) is read:

> He heard it splosh into the ditch. He backed away whimpering.

4 A third member of the class is given the role of the writer (Jamila Gavin). Position the writer in the frozen scene where you think she should be. You might use various criteria for this, including her distance from certain characters, the empathy created, the events, her intention and what control the narrator has. Justify your choice using evidence from the text to support your ideas. Discuss the positioning as a class. Throughout this discussion, other students should demonstrate the position they feel is most appropriate by moving and placing the writer and justifying their choice.

5 A fourth member of the class is given the role of the reader. Again, position the reader in the frozen scene where you think they should be. You might use various criteria for this, including the reader's distance from certain characters, the empathy felt, the events and the reader's understanding of a particular idea. Justify your choice, using evidence from the text to support your ideas. Discuss the positioning of the reader as a class. Throughout this discussion, other students should demonstrate the position they feel is most appropriate by moving and placing the reader and justifying their choice.

What have I learnt?

- How does physically placing the writer and/or reader help your understanding of the writer's perspective and techniques?
- What skills were required when deciding where to place the reader or writer and justifying your choice?
- How did the discussion and repositioning inform your understanding/thinking?
- How was empathy created in this extract? Why?

Activity 12: Placing the playwright

Learning outcomes

You will:

- analyse the adaptation process and discuss the complex decisions that are involved
- analyse the playwright's intention and techniques and explore the role of the audience in the play
- make decisions and select evidence to support your ideas.

You will do this by placing the playwright into the scene, and exploring the techniques she has used and the decisions she has made.

1   Read the following extract from the stage instructions before line 1 to the stage instructions following line 10, Act One, Scene 7 (pages 31–32):

   from   *By a dark lake on the **Ashbrook estate**.*
   to   *He quickly squats and drops her into the hole.*

2   As a class, return to the large circle. Using the space within the circle, sculpt the characters into the scene at this point in the play.

3   Discuss as a class the difficulties presented when taking the journey from script to stage. Think about how the director seeing the script for the first time would know what is meant by 'his whole being in rebellion against himself' (stage instructions following line 10, Act One, Scene 7, page 32) without having read and understood the novel. What does this say about the adaptation process? Is it the playwright or the director/actors who make the decisions about positioning, facial expressions and gestures? Does the playwright include many stage instructions?

4   A student is given the role of the playwright (Helen Edmundson). Position her where you think she should be in the frozen scene. Justify your choice, using evidence from the text to support your

ideas. Discuss the positioning as a class. Throughout the discussion, other students should demonstrate the position they feel is most appropriate by moving and placing the playwright and justifying their choice. Discuss whether this differs from the position of the writer placed in Activity 11 (page 172). Why?

5   Another student representing the audience can now be placed in the same way. Discuss the difference between placing the 'reader' and the 'audience'. Is there any? Discuss what this might tell us about the adaptation process.

What have I learnt?

- How does physically placing the playwright and audience help your understanding of the writer's perspective and techniques?
- How did this process develop your understanding of the adaptation process? What decisions do you feel the playwright had to make? Why?
- Are there aspects of the script that you would have done differently? Explain your comments by using evidence from the texts and by referring to the activities that you have completed.

Activity 13: Placing the director – dealing with the issues

Learning outcomes

You will:

- analyse the director's role in developing the play and discuss the complex decisions that are involved
- analyse the director's intention and techniques and explore the changes that are made
- make decisions and select evidence to support your decisions and ideas.

You will do this by placing the director into the scene and using **Communal Voice** to analyse the issues involved.

1   As a class, return to the sculpted images of Meshak, Otis and the writer (Activity 11).

2   A student is given the role of the director (Melly Still – Director of the National Theatre Production). Position the director in the frozen scene where you think she should be. Justify your choice, using evidence from the text to support your ideas. Discuss the positioning as a class.

3   Read the following comments adapted from the website stagework.org about why Melly Still wanted this scene to be changed. Does this change the position of the director? Why?

> Another significant change from rehearsal to performance occurred when Melly Still decided to have Otis Gardiner rather than his son Meshak physically force the still-breathing baby (Mercy) into its shallow grave. At first Meshak is seen doing this and the act makes him retch. On further reflection, Melly decided it would appear simply too much for Meshak to comply with his father at this terrible moment, not least because in the second half of the play he displays compassion by saving a baby (Melissa's) from certain death.

4   The characters remain frozen while the teacher speaks as the director:

> I do not think we should have Meshak burying the baby as he would not comply with his father at this terrible moment, not when later he shows compassion …

5   Remaining class members discuss who would speak first in response to this comment and what they would say. Would the actors respond first or would it be the playwright? When you (or another student) suggest the next line to be spoken, the characters remain frozen as you go to stand behind the person you will speak for.

6 The director's comment is read again, at the end of which you will speak the next line. Remaining class members are asked what would be said next. Individual students go and stand by the person they think they can speak for.

7 The scene is frozen again after your teacher has explained that, one by one, the people behind the sculpted actors, director or playwright will continue the scene by speaking what they say or their thoughts. Using **Communal Voice**, continue the conversation between the director, playwright and actors. What will they decide to do?

8 Read the playwright's comments about this scene in which she explains why she felt the script should not be altered – despite the director's comments. Discuss whether this affects your decision.

> I understood that Melly felt that it would be too grim for us to see Meshak burying the live baby and perhaps out of keeping with the compassion he later shows. However, I also understood why Jamila felt that this would be something Meshak had to do on numerous occasions, and that he had no choice in the matter. The fact that he vomits afterwards reflects how much this action goes against his innate humanity. Ultimately, I decided this was one of those stage directions which could be interpreted very effectively by different directors. Melly's depiction of the scene was fairly graphic, with ashen-faced babies and poignant, crying mothers, and baby Mercy took a long time to die. Another director might decide to realise the scene in a different way, which would not focus on the appalling details of the actual death, but more on the effect on Meshak of what he is forced to do. I felt it would be all right to allow people working on the play in the future to make their own decision about this.

What have I learnt?

- How does physically placing the director and playwright help your understanding of the writing and performance processes?

- How did this process develop your understanding of the adaptation process? What decisions do you feel the playwright and/or director had to make? Why?
- Are there any aspects of the script that you would have done differently? Explain your comments by using evidence from the texts and by referring to the activities that you have completed.

Activity 14: Does the writer remain? Has Jamila Gavin a role in the script and performance?

Learning outcomes

You will:

- transfer your understanding of the adaptation process of *Coram Boy* to think critically about the role of the writers in other adaptations
- analyse the relationship between writer, scriptwriter and director and the differences/similarities between the role of the reader and that of the audience
- make decisions and select evidence to support your decisions and ideas.

You will do this by considering the role of the original writer of the novel in the adapted version of the play and questioning the significance of this to the general process of adaptation.

1 Return to the sculpted scene described in Activity 12, which includes the playwright, the director and the audience. The student, who represented the writer (Jamila Gavin) in Activity 11 should stand at the side of the frozen scene. Should she be placed into the scripted scene? If so, where? Does the original writer remain part of the text? Are they left outside the scene? Are they near to the playwright or director, or do they have a different perspective? Position the writer where you feel it is most appropriate for them to be.

2 Discuss as a class whether everyone agrees with your positioning. Throughout the discussion, other students should demonstrate the position they feel is most appropriate by moving and placing the writer and justifying their choices. Discuss what this might tell us about the adaptation process. Would this be the case with all adaptations?

3 If the **Communal Voice** convention was used again, should the writer be given a voice? What would they say?

What have I learnt?

- How have the above activities helped your understanding of this particular scene and the adaptation process?
- What might the actors or director gain from taking part in similar activities?
- Who did you find most difficult to position? Why? What skills and understanding were required for this?

Activity 15: Using Rolling Theatre and Sounds to investigate the characters, atmosphere, issues and ideas

Learning Outcomes

You will:

- develop the use of space, language, facial expression and gesture
- investigate and analyse the script, selecting relevant information to explore the characters, issues and ideas
- analyse and question critically others' performances
- deduce and predict what events and themes are important in the play.

You will do this by analysing extracts from the play and making reasoned judgements about the information you are given.

1 Working in groups of three to five, you will be allocated an extract
   from the play (see below). Each group will also be given a simple
   musical instrument, such as a glockenspiel. The person with the
   musical instrument will represent Meshak 'observing' the scene
   taking place.

Extract 1: the whole of Act One, Scene 12 (pages 43 to 45) (five or six
characters)

Extract 2: opening stage instruction to line 60, Act One, Scene 18
(pages 55–57)

| from | | *Mrs Lynch and Otis enter the drawing room.* |
| to | Otis | As long as all the rest. (Two characters) |

Extract 3: lines 47–96, Act One, Scene 20 (pages 61–64)

| from | Sir William | Alexander! What are you doing out here? |
| to | Otis | Just leave him. He'll get up in a minute. (Five or six characters) |

Extract 4: the whole of Act One, Scene 31 (pages 80–83) (five or six
characters)

Extract 5: opening stage instruction to line 18, Act Two, Scene 1
(pages 87–88) and lines 33 to scene end, Act Two, Scene 2 (pages
90–91)

| from | | 1750. The **Coram Foundling Hospital**. |
| to | Govenor | ... May God be with you all. |

and

| from | Aaron | Mish! Mish! |
| to | | *Mish picks both of them up and carries them off.* (Four characters) |

Extract 6: the whole of Act Two, Scene 4 (pages 94–97) (three
characters)

Extract 7: the whole of Act Two, Scene 6 (pages 99–101) (four characters)

Extract 8: the whole of Act Two, Scene 20 (pages 127–129) (two characters)

2   Produce a short **Digital Video Clip** of your extract. Begin with a **Still Image** followed by an **Action Reading** of the script, then freeze at the end. The **Still Images** at the beginning and end of the **Digital Video Clips** should be accompanied by note(s) produced on the instrument. Think carefully about what atmosphere will be created by the note(s) your group create at the beginning and the end. How might they change? Use your note(s) to represent how the observer is feeling at the beginning and end of the scene. Think carefully about where you position the observer within your scene.

3   The extracts will be presented as **Rolling Theatre,** but you will be using a slightly different technique by adding the musical notes at the beginning and end of your clips. All the groups freeze in their initial **Still Images** and then the observer in the first group creates the note(s) on the instrument, comes to life, adds the action, then freezes again. The observer produces the sounds to accompany their final image.

4   When the first group has frozen in their final image, the next group knows that they can begin. This continues with all the groups producing their **Digital Video Clip** and punctuating their scenes with the **Still Images** and sounds until all the groups have shown their pieces.

5   When all the groups have shown their pieces and have frozen in the final image, the teacher reads lines 19–21 Act Two, Scene 9 (page 107), which are spoken in the play by Gaddarn:

> The way a nation treats its poor and unfortunate citizens, most especially its children, is a mark of how civilised it truly is.

What have I learnt?

- What skills have you used/developed in this theatrical activity?
- What have you learnt about the significance of the music and the way in which many of the scenes are 'observed'? How does this relate to other ideas and events in *Coram Boy*?
- How might the use of **Digital Video Clips** and music help your understanding of the writers' techniques in the novel and play?

Activity 16: What Meshak thinks, sees and feels – analysing the layers of meaning

Learning outcomes

You will:

- develop the use of space, facial expression and gesture
- investigate and analyse the script, selecting relevant information, and explore the use of layers of meaning and 'overheard' scenes in a production of the play
- explore a specific character and consider the actor and playwright's response to the complexity of the role.

You will do this through the production of **Still Images**, which define the important issues and ideas of a particular scene and how they might be seen differently by different characters.

1 In your groups, use the extract from Activity 15 and the information gained from producing the **Digital Video Clip** to select what you feel is the most important line from the extract.

2 Present a **Still Image** that illustrates this line and defines the important issues and ideas at this stage in the play. The image can be a literal or symbolic interpretation of the line.

3 Write the line on a large sheet of paper and place it in front of your **Still Image**. Think about how the line might be said while holding

the image. Would one character say it? Would it be said in chorus, echoed, whispered? You could use a musical instrument as well if you wanted a sound to accompany the line.

4 Now create a **Still Image** to represent Meshak's feelings if he observed that moment. Would he see and hear what is actually taking place or would he see something different? Write down on a large sheet of paper what you feel Meshak would think at that moment. Write his thoughts in the first person and place it in front of your **Still Image**. As with the line, consider how the thoughts might be said while holding the second **Still Image**. What tone or volume might you use? Decide whether you would like to add music.

5 Each group holds their first **Still Image**. The first group says their line from the extract, then gradually merges from their first **Still Image** into the **Image** that presents what Meshak sees. Then they speak Meshak's thoughts. Once they have finished, the next group will know they can begin, saying their line, merging into the second image and speaking Meshak's thoughts. This continues until all the groups have merged from one image to the other and spoken the two pieces of text.

6 Discuss as a class, the ways in which the playwright encourages us to see things through Meshak's eyes. How is the role of the observer used throughout the play?

What have I learnt?

- How did you decide on the most significant line and how this could be presented?
- How might the complex nature of the story, characters and ideas be a problem and/or benefit to the playwright and actor?
- How did this activity help you to develop your understanding of the play and the characters?

Activity 17: Music brings the characters and the beginning and ending of the play together

Before you prepare for this final activity, look back at all the headings to the activities you have done so far. Then discuss the ideas, comments and quotations collected on the stained glass angel throughout the work.

Learning outcomes

You will:

- explore the links made between the beginning and end of the play
- analyse the significance of the worlds of Gloucester, Ashbrook Estate and Coram Hospital
- use your understanding gained from all the other activities to approach the ending of the play critically and with integrity
- consider what society is
- demonstrate an understanding of the drama process.

You will do this by recreating the scenes at the beginning and end of the play in order to explore the symbolic links.

1   Sit in a semi-circle. Have with you the words given to you and object chosen for Activity 1, tasks 1 and 5 (pages 152 and 153). You should be able to see a copy of the stage instructions below from Act One, Scene 1 (page 12), which your teacher will read aloud:

> *Alexander hears and goes towards the voice. He sees Meshak staring up at his angel, singing. He watches him for a moment before answering one of Meshak's phrases, by singing a phrase himself.*

> *Meshak looks round, terrified at having been caught.*

2   One student is given the role of Meshak. Sculpt him into the position in Gloucester Cathedral you believe he will be in when the action takes place. Another student is given the role of Alexander. He is sculpted into the scene and they both freeze.

3   The teacher reads lines 21 to the stage instructions following line 25, Act Two, Scene 28 (page 146):

from   MRS HENDRY   Mr Brook? There are two boys at the door ...
to   *They reach them.*

4   Meshak remains sculpted in the earlier scene, while Alexander is resculpted, turning his back away from Meshak into this new scene in the Coram Hospital Chapel. Other students are given the roles of Melissa, Aaron and Toby. They are sculpted into the scene and all the characters freeze.

5   The characters remain frozen while the rest of the class, individually or in pairs, bring out an object used in Activity 1. As they place the object anywhere in either of the two scenes, they complete the phrase: 'Children need ...' Each student or pair places their object until they have all been placed and the statements completed.

6   The character sculpted as Alexander returns to his sculpted image with Meshak, while the other characters remain in their positions. Music (Handel's 'Messiah') may be played while your teacher reads from the stage instructions, Act One, Scene 1 (page 12):

Alexander hears and goes towards the voice. He sees Meshak staring up at the angel, singing. He watches him for a moment before answering one of Meshak's phrases, by singing a phrase himself.

Meshak looks round, terrified at having been caught. Alexander stares at him. For a moment there is a strange sense of sameness and recognition between them.

7 Alexander moves into the position he was sculpted in for the final scene and the teacher reads from the stage instructions following line 25 to line 32, Act Two, Scene 28 (pages 146–147):

from   *He turns and follows her gaze.*
to   ALEXANDER   Mish ... was your father too. But he's with the
                     angels now. He'll be your guardian angel.
                     Always.

8 All the characters remain frozen, while everyone reads out their words in the correct order to complete Gaddarn's speech following lines 19–21, Act Two, Scene 9 (page 107):

> The way a nation treats its poor and unfortunate citizens, most especially its children is a mark of how civilised it truly is.

What have I learnt?

- How have the final activities helped you to develop your understanding of the end of the play?
- What benefit might the actors or directors gain from taking part in such activities?
- Think back to the **Overheard Conversation** task in Activity 2 (page 154). Which aspects of the characters and places have remained the same and which have changed? Why?
- Has your understanding of the final quotation changed throughout the work? Why?

Reflecting on all the activities

- Which skills have you developed or learnt through this work? How will your teacher be able to tell you have learnt or developed these skills?
- Which activity do you think helped you most to enjoy, understand and/or analyse the play? Why?
- Choose two other scenes from the play and think about which drama activities or conventions you could use to explore these scenes. Explain why you would use those particular activities and what you would be expecting people to learn from them.
- Choose two of the activities, either from pages 152–185 or that you have devised, that you feel a director about to stage *Coram Boy* should use with the actors. Explain your choice and justify why you think it would be of benefit to those involved in a performance of the play.

Glossary

Action Narration a convention which requires each participant to pause and verbalise motives and descriptions of actions before they undertake them in improvisation

Action Reading students, in role, walk through a scene, speaking lines and adding gestures and movements, while reading from scripts

Communal Voice individual members of the group take up positions, one at a time, behind a sculpted character and speak the words that character says at a chosen moment in the drama; individual voices can speak more than once; a dialogue can be staged in this way with sculpted characters facing each other while their 'voices' take positions behind each of them and speak only the utterances of that character; the teacher may speak in role as one of the characters to introduce a new element or information or play devil's advocate

Conscience Alley a group divided into two lines facing each other. A pupil (or teacher) in role as a character in the drama walks between the two lines as individuals speak out what is in the character's conscience. This may be set up so that one line represents the positive aspects of the character's dilemma and the other line, the negative

Digital Video Clip a short, repeatable dramatic sequence is 'bookended' with a Still Image at the start and a Still Image at the end

Meeting Convention a group are gathered together in role to receive new information, agree action or solve problems. The meeting may be chaired by teacher in role, student in role or in some cases be deliberately convened with no identified leader

Overheard Conversation a character in the drama is identified and witnessed eavesdropping on other characters' conversations.

The device may be a means of evidencing testimony or gossip or may be a means of linking group work together as in the case of teacher in role as the eavesdropper reporting back in narration or at the end of a dramatic sequence

Placing the Author in order to help students to appreciate an author's perspective, a student or teacher represents the presence, at a defined moment in the drama, of the author; supposedly unseen by the actors (frozen at a significant moment), the author is sculpted into the scene by individual students who justify the positioning by drawing on evidence from the text; the act of placing the author is carried out as many times as demonstrates the range of possible author perspectives at any one moment in the drama

Placing the Audience/Reader a similar process to **Placing the Author** but here a student or teacher represents the presence and/or perspective of the audience or reader at a defined moment in the drama

Placing the Text participants create two paper copies of a text which could be found in a defined space in the drama. One copy is placed in the appropriate place; the other is retained by its authors. When a student/teacher in role picks up, points to or unfolds each placed text, the authors of that text read its contents out loud, providing an insight to a key character's world

Rolling Theatre a means by which groups can share their work on different aspects of a drama, learning from each other by running several rehearsed sections in a sequence; the theatrical integrity of the sequence will be the result of each group taking total responsibility for the start and finish of their section, independent of the need for teacher intervention; this may be achieved through the use of strong Still Images at the beginning and end of the Digital Video Clips signalling the contribution of the next group in a pre-arranged theatrical sequence

Role on the Object this convention is used to help students define character traits at defined moments in a drama. An object or image is placed in front of the participants. Sticky notes or cards with written statements or words are positioned by the students who have identified them on or around the object or image; students may write their own words or statements or the teacher may write them.

Sculpting participants offer suggestions to place an individual in a significant, frozen position so that considered analysis can be made

Spect-actor participants in a performed element of a drama session also become spectators and follow the action when the focus is not directly upon them. A small group might be frozen in a **Still Image** awaiting their turn to perform in a whole class drama only allowing their heads to move to spectate the action of other groups whose turn it is to perform

Still Image/Still Picture/Freeze-Frame a Still Image is created by participants in the drama standing motionless, often at a given sign by the teacher or as a result of being sculpted by other students into the frozen image. This convention is used to mark a significant moment or enable time for reflection

Tableau a multi-dimensional frozen picture usually involving a number of actors depicting a significant image

Teacher in Role a crucial technique whereby the group leader adopts a role (which could be central to the drama) that offers a model of appropriate language and behaviour. Sometimes the teacher will deliberately choose a low-status role to offer an alternative perspective